Proud Legacy

THE "COLORED" SCHOOLS OF MALVERN, ARKANSAS
AND THE COMMUNITY THAT MADE THEM

Ajuan M. Mance

Proud Legacy, Second Edition

The Henson Benson Foundation
Malvern, Arkansas

© 2012 Henson Benson Foundation

First Edition July 2012

Second Edition: February 2013

Printed in the USA

ISBN: 0985810610

ISBN 13:   9780985810610

Published by the Henson Benson Foundation

Contents

Acknowledgements

This project could not have been completed without the support of a number of hardworking and talented individuals who worked closely with me at every step of the writing and editing process. I am grateful to the filmmaker Pam Uzzell for her expertise and persistence in recording and securing transcriptions of hundreds of hours of video interviews with Malvern Colored High School and A.A. Wilson High School alumni and community members. Her support and feedback throughout the research and writing process were invaluable, and without the transcriptions of her video footage this project would not have been possible.

I am also grateful to Electra Price for her detailed research into the lives and personal histories of Taylor Henson, Tillie Yancy Benson Graham and their respective family lines. Her findings were essential to my efforts to reconstruct the history of Malvern's brick-making industry and its black business community. Thanks are due, as well, to Michael Mueller for recording my interviews with several Malvern Colored and A.A. Wilson graduates in February of 2010.

In addition to those whose research and filmmaking efforts provided so much of the primary source material for this book, I must express my heartfelt appreciation to Jewell "Pete" Willis, Jr. and Ann Spafford for their unflagging commitment to this project. I am ever indebted to them for their hard work arranging the logistics of my travel to Arkansas, my contacts with Malvern and Wilson alumni, and my access to Malvern-Wilson reunion programs, newspaper clippings, and other source material. Many thanks to Jewell Willis, who was a gracious and attentive host during my trip to Malvern; and a very special thank you to Ann Spafford, on whose organizational skills, accessibility, and experience I often relied.

I am also grateful to Laura Hunter for providing me with critical last-minute information about Malvern Colored High School and the Malvern-Wilson alumni scholarships, and to Manuel Sanchez for his cheerful optimism and unwavering commitment to preserving the rich heritage and history of the Malvern, Arkansas region. Thank you, as well, to Orval Albritton and the Hot Springs Historical Society for their time and expertise.

Additional thanks must go to Cassandra A. Falby, my partner, whose consistent support throughout this project and whose diligent work as a research and production assistant during the summer of 2010 enabled me to make rapid progress during a critical point in the creation of this volume.

Finally, I am immensely grateful to Dr. Samuel Benson, whose passion for and commitment to both preserving Malvern's history and ensuring its future was the inspiration for this book. Without his tireless work on behalf of the Henson Benson Foundation and his generous support for my research, the project would not have been possible.

Introduction

*"Remembering back now, it was just a real great time of just having some-
thing of your own and loving it."*

—Rev. Henry Mitchell, Malvern Senior
High School, Class of 1972

Every third summer since 1983, a group of African American women
and men have traveled from cities and towns across the United States, some
flying or driving and some riding buses or trains, to a small, 140-year
old community, 20 miles outside of Hot Springs. They have traveled to
Malvern, Arkansas for a very unique high school reunion. The joint all-
class reunion of the Malvern Colored and Annie A. Wilson high schools
welcomes all graduates who attended these schools to come together for a
weekend of entertainment, celebration, and praise. Though it is neither a
family reunion nor a traditional homecoming weekend, this event incorpo-
rates several elements of each. Many in attendance bring their spouses, their
children, and their grandchildren to join in the festivities as they celebrate
the joys of lifelong friendship and enduring school pride. The Malvern-
Wilson reunion is a time for old friends and classmates to reconnect, to
share cherished memories of favorite classes and beloved teachers, to reminisce about the football games and homecoming parades, and to honor the
community that supported them.

Of course, the Malvern-Wilson all-class reunion is not the only gathering of graduates that draws attendees from across the U.S., nor is it the only
alumni gathering that brings together former students from all classes.
Indeed, high schools and colleges around the country hold similar gatherings, annually, or less frequently, as in the case of the Malvern event. Still,
the joint reunion of the Malvern Colored and A.A. Wilson high schools

stands apart from more conventional reunion events because the attendees represent an entire school system (as opposed to one specific high school) and, even more uniquely, because the attendees are African American alumni of a racially segregated school system that was dissolved many decades ago. Malvern Colored High School graduated its first class of high school seniors in 1945. Relocated in 1951 to a new building and renamed for a skilled and beloved schoolteacher, Annie Agnes (A.A.) Wilson High School graduated its last class in 1968, the year that Malvern integrated its public schools.

During the 23 years in which Malvern maintained a separate African American high school program, Arkansas was one of 17 states and the District of Columbia in which black students were required by state and local law to attend school separate from their white counterparts. Universally condemned by anti-racist activists during and after the Jim Crow era, legally enforced racial segregation lives in the U.S. public memory as a great national shame, alongside North American chattel slavery and Native American genocide. Thus, many outside of the Malvern area might find it puzzling that a group of African American men and women would return so faithfully, and often at great expense, to celebrate two schools whose very existence is seen by many as emblematic of the divisive racial climate of the Jim Crow South. For the graduates of Malvern Colored and A.A. Wilson, however, the memory of these African American high schools resonates not with the pain of exclusion, but with the pride of ownership and belonging. The story of these high schools and the achievements of their graduates challenge much of the conventional wisdom surrounding the education of African Americans in the pre-civil rights era South. The loyal cadre of alumni who have returned, reunion after reunion, to celebrate and remember their teachers and their schools bears witness to the simple but little understood fact that segregated education was not always substandard.

The Malvern-Wilson alumni, through their many achievements in the years since graduation, have demonstrated that the quality of a given school system owes more to the dedication of its teachers and the support of its community than to questions of wealth, facilities, or the local tax base. Malvern Colored and A.A. Wilson were small high schools in what was then a small city (only 8,072 residents in 1950); and each was a far cry from the regional and comprehensive high schools now common throughout Arkansas. In fact, Malvern Colored High School's first graduating class was comprised of only 7 students; and, together, the high schools existed as a full secondary program for just under a quarter century before the teachers and students of A.A. Wilson were absorbed into the larger and previously whites-only system. Yet, in this short span of time, Malvern's small "colored" high schools produced a number and range of professionals—physicians, journalists, attorneys, judges, teachers, professors, shop owners, politicians, full-time parents, actors, members of the clergy, and community leaders—more commonly associated with elite public or private preparatory programs.

In their own achievements and in the achievements of their children and grandchildren, the Malvern-Wilson alumni bear witness to the greatest triumph of Malvern's black high schools, their effectiveness at instilling in their students both a faith in their own abilities and an understanding of the community's expectation that all would succeed. In so doing, Malvern Colored and A.A. Wilson provided the type of strong educational foundation that was generally available only to white students from economically and socially privileged backgrounds, but to a small-town, southern, African American population for whom such advantages were rarely reserved.

The rich legacy of Malvern's African American schools is the subject of this book. This volume traces the rise of the region's African American community from its earliest origins, during slavery, to the present day. Although the tale begins in Arkansas, it will extend far beyond the boundaries of the state, as it traces the movements and achievements of Malvern's graduates, whose educational and professional goals have carried them literally from one coast of the United States to the other. (Today there are active Malvern-Wilson alumni groups not only in Arkansas, but in Northern and Southern California, as well.)

In reconstructing the story of Malvern's African American schools, this book draws on a number of sources, including newspaper clippings, Works Progress Administration interview transcripts, scholarly and critical tracts, electronic media, reference volumes, and current and historic state maps. The most important sources by far, though, are the voices of the Malvern and Wilson alumni themselves. The classrooms, teachers, friendships, cafeteria meals, and marching band performances at Malvern Colored and A.A. Wilson high schools live on in the memories of their graduates; and the words of the Malvern-Wilson alumni, culled from hundreds of hours of interviews conducted and videotaped by Pam Uzzell, with assistance from

Ajuan Mance and Michael Mueller, give structure and substance to the story that unfolds in the following chapters.

This book follows the growth of Malvern's African American community and the rise of its "colored" school system and then moves on to explore some of the factors that contributed to Malvern Colored and A.A. Wilson's unusual success in preparing its graduates for post-secondary study and eventual employment. The memories of Malvern Colored and A.A. Wilson graduates play a central role in answering the "what" of this book, as alumni recall not only the teachers, staff members, and administrators that defined the African American experience of segregated education in the Malvern and Perla region, but also the families, neighborhoods, businesses, and industries that sustained them. It is, however, in addressing the question of why Malvern was able to develop and sustain such a successful African American school system during the Jim Crow era that this volume turns to more traditional critical and historical sources. Why, among the many small southern towns that offered secondary education to black youth, was Malvern able to provide not merely an adequate education, but an exceptional one? In pursuing these questions, this volume examines the economic, geographic, and financial conditions in Hot Spring and neighboring Garland counties as well as the political culture, faith communities, and racial climate in the region during the decades of segregation, alone as well as in comparison with other counties across the state.[1]

As such, the story of Malvern's black schools is inextricable from the black history of Malvern itself; and the black history of Malvern is as much the story of a region and its people—all of its people, across races—as it is of the fortunes of a single, clearly defined ethnic and cultural group. Indeed, the history of Malvern and its schools reveals an area in which relationships between black and white people and their communities were significantly less contentious than in other parts of Arkansas. Indeed, it is impossible to understand the legacy of Malvern's "colored" schools without examining the racial climate of the region. Although the focus of this book is on the extraordinary history of the black education system in the decades before integration, the growth and success of Malvern's African American community and its schools depended on the ability of the town's black and white communities to live and work side-by-side, this in a region (west-central Arkansas) that has become noted for a greater level of racial tolerance and considerably less tension between ethnic and racial groups than in other parts of state.

The racial legacy of west-central Arkansas is, in many ways, embodied in the figure of President William Jefferson Clinton, whose comfort with African American people, familiarity with U.S. black cultural practices, and commitment to expanding opportunities for both the state and the nation's black residents led the African American novelist Toni Morrison to refer to him as the "first black president" of the United States.[2] Raised in and around the towns of Hope and Hot Springs, Arkansas, Clinton came of age during the decades before integration, in the somewhat more tolerant and significantly less violent racial atmosphere that characterized the region, which also includes Malvern and neighboring Perla. As the Governor of Arkansas, his west-central Arkansas heritage was evident in his diligent work to create growth and prosperity for the disproportionately poor and undereducated African American population of his home state. As President of the United States, Clinton brought to the national and international stage the racially inclusive sensibility that, as a child of Hope and Hot Springs, was his birthright.

The coming-of-age of the Malvern Colored and A.A. Wilson graduates paralleled developments in the economic and cultural fortunes of Malvern's black community at large, just as events in the larger history of Malvern's black community shaped and were shaped by the changes and developments in Malvern's black schools. As such, the story of Malvern Colored and A.A. Wilson and their alumni is not only a tale of teachers, parents, and communities joined together to insure the success of their youth. It is also the story of the changes wrought by migration and loss; and yet even in terms of the now familiar narrative of black migration—from racism and poverty in the South to greater tolerance and opportunity in the North— the Malvern-Wilson story is unique. Books like historian Isabel Wilkerson's The Warmth of Other Suns and novelist James Baldwin's Go Tell It on the Mountain portray black northern migration as necessitated by the desire to escape Jim Crow segregation and pervasive racial violence.[3] Though racially segregated, Malvern was largely free from the terroristic attacks that devastated the lives of so many black families in the pre-civil rights era South. So too were employment opportunities in Malvern and neighboring Perla greater and more diverse than was common in all but the South's largest cities. Migration from Malvern occurred much later than in many other small southern towns, and for different reasons. Indeed, those who sought baccalaureate and post-graduate degrees made up a disproportionate number of Malvern's emigrants. Thus the strong academic foundation provided by Malvern schools is, ironically, a critical part of the story of this community's northern migration story.

In a region in which the fortunes of black residents, though not identical, were more similar to those of their white counterparts than in other parts of the south, it should come as no surprise that, even as we are tempted to link the migration of black people from Malvern to the storied Great Migration that has been the subject of so many documentaries and scholarly tracts, the concerns and conditions that inspired the northern and westward migration of Malvern Colored and A.A. Wilson graduates were more closely linked to those which precipitated the similar but less widespread migration of many post-World War II white families from small southern towns. These factors include both the lack of broad opportunities for those with baccalaureate and post-baccalaureate degrees and the impact of the exodus of degree-holding residents on local businesses and home values.

Despite this, however, the story of Malvern Colored and A.A. Wilson high schools, their alumni, and the communities that fostered them is not as much a desperate chronicle of outward migration as it is a tale of triumphant return, reflected in both the continued attraction of Malvern for the many alumni who remained and built their lives in that community and the cyclical return of those alums who now make their homes elsewhere. When the Malvern Colored and A.A. Wilson graduates return for their triennial all-class reunions, they come to rekindle old friendships and to recognize and honor the memory of those teachers, principals, coaches, cooks, and other staff members who built and sustained Malvern's black schools. Most significantly though, this gathering of alumni, assembled from points near and far, is a reassertion of identity and belonging. With his or her presence at the reunion, each returning alum affirms that wherever he or she may live, and however many years may have passed since that fateful graduation day, a Malvern Colored High School Leopard will always be a Leopard and a Wilson Dragon will always be a Dragon. For all of the returning alumni—and for those who are unable to make the trip to Malvern, but who are present in spirit—these schools, whose memories they carry in their hearts and their minds, will forever feel like home.

Chapter I

A Land of Opportunity: The Early Black History of Malvern

"Everyone knows that a sharecropper is going to be a sharecropper all of his life. He's never going to be able to pay and get out from under being a sharecropper. But here's a place where you can go and earn enough money to take care of your family"

—Dr. Samuel Benson, Malvern Colored
High School, Class of 1952

In 1945, the first seven seniors graduated from the high school program at Malvern Colored School. Few who were present at this occasion, however, could have known that the pathway to this moment began nearly 100 years before they were born, with a series of developments in the region's agricultural and industrial landscape that precipitated the slow-but-steady growth of its region's black population. Indeed, any discussion of the extraordinary legacy of Malvern Colored and A.A. Wilson high schools must necessarily begin with the history of Malvern's African American community; and to understand that history is to understand the intimate relationship between black labor in and black migration to the region.

The African American community of Malvern, Arkansas achieved its greatest levels of growth and expansion during the period between the end of Reconstruction and the beginning of World War I, when free black families were seeking employment opportunities that would grant them

1

greater autonomy and stability than tenant farming (sharecropping) and other forms of agricultural labor. This chapter explores some of the developments that transformed Malvern into a preferred destination for black migrants from throughout the south.

Unlike Virginia, North Carolina, and other coastal states of the South, Arkansas did not begin to see any significant growth in its African American community until after the formal cessation of the Atlantic slave trade, in 1808. In fact, in 1829, 11 years after the U.S. had formally ceased the importation of black labor from Africa, there were fewer than 2000 enslaved African Americans living and working in Arkansas territory.[4] Compare this to Virginia, which by 1750 had amassed a population of more than 200,000 black slaves. The soil and climate in Virginia, North Carolina, South Carolina, and Georgia were ideal for growing cotton, tobacco, sugarcane, and rice, the nation's most lucrative agricultural products at that time. Labor-intensive and grueling to cultivate, these crops were raised on farms and plantations that required a number of workers in order to remain profitable. Though Arkansas would eventually become the nation's sixth largest producer of cotton, the production and trade in this valuable commodity was never as deeply entrenched in the state as it was in some of its older, eastern counterparts.

Arkansas' unique relationship to the cultivation of cotton and other cash crops was due, in part, to the fact that the first significant wave of European settlers did not arrive in the territory that would become the state of Arkansas until 1819, a full 200 years after the Europeans first established Virginia's Jamestown colony. Of equal importance, however, is Arkansas' distinctive geography. Endowed with natural resources that yielded their products without cultivation, the Arkansas economy relied more heavily on industries like tourism, brick making, and lumber than most other southern economies and, in many cases, decades earlier than in Virginia, the Carolinas, Georgia, Mississippi, and Alabama. Add to this the fact that certain portions of the state had clay soil, mountainous terrain or other geological features that were inhospitable to the cultivation of cotton, tobacco, cane, rice, and other cash crops, and the reason for the slow growth of slavery in the state becomes clear.

Consequently, while small groups of black slaves lived in Arkansas during the early 1800s, it was not until the middle of the century that the numbers of African Americans in the state began to increase significantly.

Among that small number of enslaved black men and women who were brought to the Malvern and Perla area during the earliest decades of the 19th century were Crawford and Lucinda Williams, the grandparents of retired schoolteacher and lifelong Malvern resident Lendora Williams Miles. In an interview published in About Our People: The Black History of Malvern, she recalls that her grandparents "were born in Charlotte, North Carolina and were brought to Arkansas as slaves by Colonel Daniel Morrison, who settled on land near the Ouachita River in Saginaw, a small community in Hot Spring [County], during the early 1800s."[5] Crawford and Lucinda Williams were the great-grandparents of Marva Jasper, Wilson High School Class of 1966.

Just as Arkansas' relatively late entry into the production of cash crops delayed the spread of slavery within its borders, so too did the absence of cotton plantations in the area that would eventually become Malvern and Perla result in significantly less demand for slave labor in that region than in other portions of the state.[6] In addition, the small-scale farming and domestic labor into which Malvern and Hot Springs area slaves were pressed led to a form of bondage that, although no less reprehensible a violation of black people's fundamental human rights, was characterized by somewhat less tension, less violence, and more humanizing conditions and interactions between the enslaved black people and their white owners than was common in the state's cotton belt. The following excerpt from an interview with City of Hot Springs resident Warren Taylor, whose mother was enslaved by Charlie Adams and Mack Adams of Malvern, supports this perspective. Part of a Works Progress Administration (WPA) effort to preserve the memories of the formerly enslaved, this interview, recorded during the early 1930s, suggests that at least some Malvern area slave owners were able to cultivate a modicum of respect for their black laborers. Taylor offers this recollection:

> The Adamses were good to my mother. And they helped her even after freedom. Charlie Adams and Mack Adams of Malvern, Arkansas. John was the sheriff and ran a store. Mack was a drummer for the Penzl Grocery. When my mother was ill, he used to bring her thirty dollars at a time. Every two months she had to go down to Malvern when she was well and carry an empty trunk and when she would come back it would

be full. My mother was wet-nurse to the Adamses and they thought the world and all of her.[7]

A pivotal moment in the development of the area's black community came on June 13, 1859, when the Rev. Balm W. Whitlow and eight enslaved African Americans founded New Hope Baptist Church on the banks of the Ouachita River. The enslaved men and women who gathered together for worship did so in secret. WPA Federal Writers Project interviewee James Reeves describes the risks and struggles endured by his Malvern area slave ancestors in order to practice their faith, as they were recounted to him by Rev. Whitlow himself:

> Old man Balm Whitlow can tell you all about the way that they held church. They would slip off in the woods and carry a gang of darkies down, and the next morning old master would whip them for it. Next Sunday they would do the same thing again and get another whipping. And it went on like that every week. When old man Whitlow came of out slavery, he continued to preach. But the darkies didn't have to steal out then.[8]

Among those eight enslaved men and women to whom Whitlow preached were the grandparents of Lendora Miles. After the arrival of freedom, Miles's grandparents and the remainder of their group elected Whitlow as their first pastor, and they began the task of constructing a more permanent space of worship. Miles's grandparents were among those newly-freed men and women who cut down the trees that were used to build the church's first structure, which they called a *brush arbor*. They named their church the New Hope Baptist Church "because," Lendora Miles explains, "God had given them new hope and a new lease on life with their freedom."[9] Descendants of two of the founding members of New Hope, Lendora Miles and her sister Eva, have each been active in New Hope Baptist for nearly half of the more than 140-year history of that institution. Both are "gold star members" of the church, with each having served their congregation for roughly 70 years.

The end of U.S. slavery, in January of 1863, brought additional transformations both to the Malvern area and to the lives of those who made it their home. When slavery ended in the region that would become Malvern,

Arkansas, many of its formerly enslaved black men and women were able to transition into paid work, as domestic laborers in the homes of white merchants, as laborers in its growing natural resources-based industries, and as workers on a new and significant project that would transform the lives and fortunes of the entire region, the "Diamond Jo" railroad.

While Virginia, the Carolinas, Georgia, Louisiana, Mississippi and other southern states sought economic stability through agriculture, significant portions of Arkansas were able not only to survive, but to thrive and grow based on the development of non-agrarian industries and an industrialized labor force. This was especially true of the west-central portion of the state, where the city of Hot Springs and surrounding communities like Malvern, Perla, Hope, and Rockport were able to take advantage of the geologically rich landscape to develop an alternative economic structure based on wage labor in stable and climate-resistant businesses and trades. For the city of Hot Springs, located in adjacent Garland County, this meant the development of a vibrant and prosperous tourism industry, based on its natural hot and cold springs. Indeed, one of the most important developments in the economy of the region took place in 1832, when, in response to a request by the Arkansas Territorial Legislature, the U.S. Congress created the Hot Springs Reservation, a move that granted federal protections to the region's famous healing waters.

It is a testament to the appeal of its waters that, throughout the middle of the 1800s, the tourism industry in Hot Springs was able to thrive, despite the absence of any major transit lines into the popular destination. Stage coach travel to the area began in 1836, a mode of transportation that was complicated by the rutted and mountainous terrain that led into the city. Access to Hot Springs improved significantly in the early 1870s, when the St. Louis & Iron Mountain Railroad established service to nearby Malvern. Visitors were able to travel by rail coach to Malvern station, only 24 miles away, at which point they could board a transport operated by one of the regional stage coach lines for the long and rutted road to Hot Springs.

As dangerous as it was rugged, the passage from Malvern to Hot Springs was plagued by gangs of highwaymen who would lay in wait for the regularly scheduled caravans run by El Paso and Independent, the area's two major stage coach operators. On January 15, 1874, the outlaw Jesse James and his gang overtook an El Paso line stage coach as it traveled the Malvern to Hot Springs route. Dressed in the blue wool coats of Union soldiers, members of the James Gang escaped with more than 800 dollars in cash and other valuables.

Many visitors to Hot Springs were ill or infirm and seeking a cure in the city's therapeutic baths. For these travelers, the discomfort and danger of stage coach travel posed a particular hazard, best captured in this 1875 quote from a visitor to the region who observed that, "it seems almost a miracle that some of [the ill and infirm visitors] survive the stage ride over the rough and dangerous road to the springs."[10] The arrival of the Diamond Jo railroad line in 1876 greatly improved traveling conditions and safety for all of those who sought to make the overland trip from Malvern to Hot Springs. Linking the renowned spa city to the St. Louis & Iron Mountain railroad line, by way of Malvern Station, the Diamond Jo increased the profile of the smaller neighboring city as the junction through which all travelers to the state's most storied resort town were forced to pass. Originally constructed as a narrow gauge railway, this line was built by Chicago millionaire and industrialist "Diamond Jo" Reynolds. Reynolds suffered from rheumatism, and his backing for the project was rumored to have been motivated by his desire for a safer, more pleasant mode of transportation on his frequent trips to enjoy Hot Springs' curative waters.[11]

The popularity of the Diamond Jo brought in its wake a new level of status for Malvern. Little more than a train depot and stage coach hub surrounded by a small number of supporting businesses, Malvern was incorporated as a city on July 22, 1876. On October 15 of 1878, the newly appointed city was named the Hot Spring County seat (the city of Hot Springs is the county for neighboring Garland County). In 1887, the Malvern Roundhouse was built to house the servicing and repair operations for the region's rail lines, a move that further established the city as the industrial, commercial, and transport center of the county.

By 1899, Malvern had come to be known throughout much of the state not only as a transportation hub, but also as a regional center for commerce and manufacturing. That year's *National Newspaper Directory and Gazetteer* described Malvern as a "trading centre for [a] farming and manufacturing region with 5000 pop."[12] Turn-of-the-century Malvern was home to the Clark Pressed Brick Company, the Malvern Lumber Company, and Malvern Tile & Pottery; and its flourishing industries made it a preferred destination for those seeking greater economic opportunity, including many black individuals and families from other parts of Arkansas and throughout the south.

By 1900, African American families who migrated to Malvern had begun to settle in the area called Barnett Addition. Later known as the neighborhood "Across the Creek," this section was located between Barnett Street and Walco Road, adjacent to but not yet incorporated into Malvern's city limits.[13] Migration to the city—and to the neighboring community of Perla—continued long past the turn of the last century, through the first World War, the Great Depression, and World War II; and many Malvern and Wilson alumni attribute their families' arrival in the area to the search for a stable income and dignified work. The grandparents of Alvin Murdoch (Malvern Senior High School, Class of 1968) moved to Malvern from the Dallas County area, but left Malvern in the hope of finding even greater opportunity in Little Rock. Recalls Murdoch, "There were more opportunities [here], and they came back to Malvern."[14] Jimmy Hunter (Wilson High School, Class of 1966) migrated to Malvern after World War II, with his immediate family and members of his extended family, all of whom were attracted to the greater economic prospects that awaited them in this industrial center. He explains that, "the jobs were in Malvern, and my uncles and aunties all moved here first."[15]

The family of Marva Jasper was attracted not only to the number of jobs that were available in the Malvern area, but also to the kind of labor for which African Americans were being hired. Many of the first black families who migrated to the city sought industrial labor as a more economically and personally rewarding alternative to sharecropping and other forms of agricultural work. In this excerpt from a recent interview, Marva explains that, "A lot of people migrated into Malvern as a result of the different industries that we had located here in the area … A lot of them were farming because Arkansas is a farm state."[16] Among those migrants who sought greater prospects in the city was her father. Originally from the Camden area in Ouachita County, Jasper's father "settled in Malvern … at the end of World War II, when he got out of the Army."[17] Also from the Camden area were the parents and grandparents of Laura Hunter (Wilson High School, Class of 1964), who moved to Malvern from Ogemaw, Arkansas, also in Ouachita County. "They came here," she explains, "because my grandfather did not want to farm anymore. They had a farm, they had their own land, but he just didn't want the farm anymore; so he came here to work—and he actually started working on the railroad."[18]

For African Americans in the pre-civil rights era South, the opportunity to leave farm labor behind brought with it the freedom to strive for upward mobility, if not for themselves, then certainly for their children and grandchildren. While wage labor in the industries that fueled Malvern's early economy provided sufficient income for black and white families alike to build homes, feed their extended families, and educate their children, sharecropping and other tenant farmer arrangements that were common in other Arkansas cities and towns ensnared black laborers in a cycle of endless debt that thwarted any attempts to provide more than a subsistence living for their dependents. "Many of the people who came to Malvern came from places not too far away, but they were sharecroppers," explains Dr. Samuel Benson. "A sharecropper's never going to be able to pay and get out from under being a sharecropper," but Malvern was "a place where you [could] earn enough money to take care of your family.[19]

Despite its small size (in 1932, the population of Malvern was "just over 5000," up from 1582 in 1900), Malvern's industrial base was not only booming, but also quite broad. The city was able to provide employment for most of its residents not only because work was plentiful, but also because the range of industries in the region could accommodate the skills and abilities of a diverse population of workers. The relationship between Malvern's local industries and the African American community comes into sharp focus through the recollections of Malvern Colored and Wilson High School alumni, many of whose parents and grandparents earned a living transforming the area's natural resources—timber, clay, and bauxite—into valuable commodities.

Lumber

Lumber milling, the region's oldest industry, became a dominant force in the rapidly developing economy of the Malvern area, beginning in the late 1800s. The privately owned sawmills and their associated logging operations were attracted to the heavily forested areas of west-central Arkansas, including the Ouachita Mountains, which run west from Hot Springs, across the state border and into Oklahoma.[20] Malvern Lumber was the oldest mill in the area and one of the first private milling operations established in the state. Founded in 1880, when German immigrant Adalbert Strauss built a sawmill just east of the city limits, Malvern Lumber attracted laborers from across the region. These new migrants to Hot Spring County created a small settlement adjacent to the mill, for themselves and their families. Strauss named this community Perla, after his daughter Perla Ann.

The Malvern Lumber Company expanded rapidly during its first three decades, operating the narrow gauge Perla, Magnet & Pacific Railroad in the 1890s and establishing an additional rail line, the Perla Northern, in 1904.[21] The company experienced a pivotal setback in 1918, when fire destroyed its single-band mill. Malvern Lumber rebuilt, but on a significantly smaller scale. The final blow to the company came in 1929, when the arrival of the Great Depression sounded a death knell for manufacturing and processing plants across the nation. According to Ed Green (Wilson High School, Class of 1959), the Malvern Lumber Company had shut down most of its operations by 1930, when its directors held their last meeting. In the coming decades, the company would gradually distribute its assets to other larger lumber and paper products processing and manufacturing ventures. Local businessman and timber executive Larry Parker recalls that, after Malvern Lumber closed its logging and milling operations, "they sold over the years about 15,000 acres to Weyerhaeuser Corporation in the same county ... And then Georgia Pacific Corporation bought the rest of it, which was about a total of 5000 acres, in 1969."[22]

Malvern Lumber Company also distributed some of its assets to its former employees. Larry Parker remembers that a curious side-effect of the company's collapse was that it resulted in a number of area residents being able to build their first homes:

> [W]hen they shut down, of course, Malvern Lumber Company owed people money and stuff, wages ... they gave them some little plots of land ... people put houses on some of them and some of them are just grown up in woods. But they gave the little house sites for the money that they owed them for working at the mills, because the banks [collapsed, and] they didn't have money to pay them with.[23]

Other area lumber companies suffered a similar fate, most without such generous attempts to arrive at a fair wage and property settlement with employees. The Arkansas Land and Lumber Company closed its Malvern mills in 1929.

The closing of Malvern Lumber and Arkansas Land and Lumber did not mean the end of that industry's influence on the area economy. New lumber and wood products companies would continue to be attracted to the region well past the middle of the 20th century. The Sturgis Lumber Company began production at its Malvern plant in 1938, with Weyerhaeuser, Georgia Pacific, and International Paper establishing operations during the next several decades. The latter three companies maintain a presence in Malvern to this day.

The lumber mills hired a diverse range of men, representing the full range of ethnic groups, ages, and abilities. Samuel Bryant (Wilson High School, Class of 1968) recalls that his father was able to find stable, reliable work at the sawmill, despite having only one eye. Not only was his father able to earn a steady income in the lumber industry, but he was also well-respected for his skill and hard work. Samuel Bryant still remembers the "happy occasion" of his father's retirement from International Paper, at which he received a reclining chair as a gift of appreciation.[24]

African American employees held many types of positions at the Malvern and Perla lumber mills. Ed Green recalls that many members of the region's black community were employed as "billet haulers." A billet, he explains, was "a relatively short piece of a tree."[25] This job was an essential one because, he explains, "I don't recall there being a whole lot of log trucks or log haulers at that time, nothing like there is today."[26] Some mill employees were responsible for cutting timber. Laura Hunter's father was among those who were employed in the woods, cutting the timber that others would process into usable wood products. "My father came to Malvern for work," she explains, "and he initially began working in the woods. We called it the billet woods [and] they would cut trees and load the trees manually on the trucks and haul the trees out."[27] Other workers were assigned the task of transporting the logs to the mill. In a 2011 interview conducted near one of the old mill sites, Ed Green explained the process of bringing the logs from the log pond to their final destination before milling:

[The lumber company] had a railroad where I'm standing now, a spur that came off of this main line. It wasn't near this big then, and came down through here, and they dumped their logs up here in the mill pond, and then rails came right through here and they'd load lumber on here and ship it back out along to the main line. And they brought the logs from the log pond up here under the county road here ... It all run off of steam. And the creek that comes under the railroad here now went literally under the mill. And they used the water from the creek to get the water to run their steam power unit.[28]

Aluminum

The aluminum industry came to Malvern in 1941. U.S. involvement in World War II pushed the nation's demand for aluminum to unprecedented levels. Home to some of the nation's largest reserves of bauxite, the rocky ore from which aluminum is refined, Arkansas became a centerpiece in the federal government's defense strategy. In 1941 the U.S. War Department launched a plan to build defense plants across Arkansas, including a substantial reduction operation at the Jones Mills plant, seven miles northeast of Malvern. After the war, the Reynolds Company purchased the Jones Mills plant and continued to maintain its operations into the 1980s.[29]

Physically demanding and often dangerous, work at the aluminum plant nonetheless paid more than many jobs at the lumber mill and in the region's third major industry, brick production. When long-time Malvern resident Ed Green was a young man seeking good, stable work with relatively high wages, he looked immediately to the aluminum industry. Green recalls "having as kind of a standard goal ... to get a job or wind up with a job that paid one hundred dollars a week, because that's ... what the guys from Reynolds were earning."[30] These high wages, however, came in exchange for considerably more hazardous working conditions than in either the brick or lumber industries. Green sums up this trade-off, noting that wages at the aluminum reduction plant were, "a significant step up for a lot of folk, if you were able to deal with the heat and the dust and the dirt and all the rest of the stuff that went along with it."[31] He remembers the conditions at Reynolds as "tough ... because of the heat." It was also "dirty" and "dusty"; but, more than anything, Green recalls the work as "hot, and more hot."[32]

The hot, dusty environment in the aluminum plant adversely affected the health of many workers. Ed Green remembers, "People used to regularly do what they call burn out, which is a phrase that they had if you became overheated, [if] you were something just shy of having a heatstroke … you would just get exhausted from the heat and literally almost pass out or get very faint, anyway."[33] Judy Pierce (Malvern Senior High School, Class of 1969) says, "I remember my dad worked for Reynolds aluminum plant when I was very young, and he worked there until he got sick and he died in … 1949."[34]

The high wages at Jones Mills and, later, at the Reynolds aluminum plant were partially attributable to the era in which that industry saw its greatest development in the region. Having arrived in the city in the 1940s, more than 50 years after the first sawmills and 40 years after the first brick plants, the aluminum industry benefitted from the high market value of its product, relative to lumber and bricks. Wages at the Jones Mills plant were also, to a greater or lesser extent, following the precedent set by the brick industry, which was able to attract hard-working and able-bodied laborers of all ethnicities in part because of its stated promise to pay all of its employees the same wage for the same work, regardless of race.

Brick

The *Encyclopedia of Arkansas* describes Malvern as, "by far the leading city in brick production in Arkansas."[35] Rich in clay deposits suitable for brick making, the city began its rise to prominence as one of the premier brick production centers of the nation in 1890, when the Atchison brick plant began operations in the city. Atchison Brick Works was followed by many other brick production plants, including the Clark Pressed Brick Company, Malvern Brick and Tile, and Arkansas Brick and Tile, which acquired the Atchison plant in 1917. In the lives of Malvern's black residents, however, the single most important development in the growth of the early brick industry was set in motion by Malvern transplant Taylor Henson.

The story of Taylor Henson's pivotal involvement in the region's brick industry begins with his seemingly uncanny ability to purchase tracts of land that were strategically important to the region's growing industrial and transportation needs. A former slave, Henson was a land investor and speculator who amassed significant property holdings in Malvern and Perla. Born in Hot Springs, Arkansas in 1850, Henson migrated to Malvern in the late 1800s, ready to invest in its land and natural resources. When he arrived in Malvern, "he brought right smart money with him, and he had it rolled up with a rubber band over it," recalls his granddaughter, long-time Perla resident and business-owner, Frances Calhoun.[36]

A critical part of Henson's investment strategy was to purchase undeveloped land that others believed to be useless or impractical for farming. "[H]e bought land that others said was too close to the Ouachita river and therefore would be flooded...and he bought it very cheaply," recalls great-grandson Dr. Samuel Benson. Through this tactic, Henson was able to acquire vast holdings of fertile farmland that was easy to irrigate. "[H]e was able to manipulate the land in such a way that it produced corn, which was his first crop, in abundance," explains Dr. Benson, adding that, eventually, Henson's "cantaloupes and watermelons became so important" that he was able to use the area's railways to find markets for his produce as far away as Chicago and the East Coast.[37]

By the beginning of the 1920s, Taylor Henson had established a reputation for purchasing large tracts of Malvern area real estate, but never selling. In fact, the May 1917 issue of The Crisis, the NAACP's official magazine and one of the oldest African American periodicals in the United States, ran an article on Henson titled "The Man Who Never Sold an Acre."[38] Ironically, it was only two years later that Henson did, in fact, sell a number of acres, in a real estate transaction that would set a critical precedent in the relationship of the region's industries to its African American workers. In 1919, Taylor Henson sold 120 acres of land in Perla, Arkansas, immediately adjacent to the city of Malvern, to Walter R. Bennett, then president of the Texas-based Acme Brick Company. If Taylor Henson's greatest contribution to the economy of the Malvern region had been securing the land deal that led to the local expansion of the Acme Brick Company, then that accomplishment in and of itself would certainly have earned him a respected place in Malvern history. It was, however, his shrewd negotiation of the terms of this land deal with Acme that most dramatically and most personally touched the lives of the area's African American residents. Henson offered to sell a portion of his land to the Acme Brick Company for a very reasonable sum, but only on the condition that the corporation would pay its black employees at a rate equal to that which they paid white employees who held the same position. Explains Dr. Samuel Benson, "they had to promise him that whomever they hired to do the work there would be paid on the basis of what they did, and not on the basis of their skin color."[39]

Acme's Malvern-Perla plant began full operations in 1921; and in that very same year, this, the largest company in the city's dominant industry, hired its African American employees at the same rate at which it compensated its white workers, a full 43 years before Title VII of the Federal Equal Pay Act mandated equal pay for comparable work, regardless of the race or ethnicity of the worker. While not all of the other industries in Malvern and Perla embraced this practice at the time, Henson's skillfully negotiated land deal set an important precedent for the treatment and compensation of black workers in the region, a move that reinforced and expanded Malvern's reputation as a place of opportunity for individuals and families of African descent.

In the decades since their arrival in Malvern, the Acme Brick Company has continued to grow, beginning in 1926, when it purchased both the Atchison Brick Works and Arkansas Brick and Tile. Even as it has grown, however, the company has never forgotten its promise to Taylor Henson. In 2001, as part of its celebration of 80 years in the Malvern-Perla area, Acme Brick Company leaders invited Frances Calhoun, Henson's granddaughter, to participate in the festivities. Henson's great-grandson, Dr. Benson, still remembers that representatives of the company assured his mother, Mrs. Calhoun, that Acme Brick "never went against the promise they made to Taylor." In that same ceremony, Acme representatives awarded Dr. Benson and his mother "the bricks to the city."[40]

Like the jobs at the aluminum plant, work in the brick yards of Malvern and Perla was physically demanding. The rigor of the work was, however, offset by the generosity of the wages that the industry paid its laborers. "[A]t one time," recalls Jewell "Pete" Willis, a long-time Malvern resident, "if you really wanted to work the brick yard, you was making more than anybody else in the community."[41] The most challenging jobs at the plant offered the highest pay. Ed Green explains:

> People would do what they would call contract. I don't really understand all that that meant, but the little bit that I do recall from it,

they would be charged with loading up so many boxcars of bricks, and if they did that in the given amount of time, then they would of course be compensated pretty nicely for that. But that was some very hard and backbreaking work.[42]

Jewell Willis echoes Green's assessment of contract work as difficult, but lucrative, noting that, "Some of the guys were making really good money ... some of the guys [doing] contract work, they was making $100 a week, but they worked for it—worked very hard for it."[43] Contract labor may have been the most difficult and exhausting way to earn a living at the plant but, in reality, there were few positions at the brick yard that were not physically exhausting. Recalls Ed Green, "All of the work associated with the brickyard was hard work."[44] For some young men, a stint at the brick yard was all the inspiration they needed to become more focused on preparing for life after high school. "If you could get on a summer job at the brick plant," Jewell Willis explains, "that'll help you decide you want to go to the military or you really want to go to college, one of the two."[45]

White and black workers did not always perform the same work at the brick yard. Willis recalls, "The whites had the best jobs, the easiest jobs," and the blacks were frequently in the position of "taking the jobs that the whites didn't want." Still, when white and black men did the same work, they were paid the same wages, thanks to the legacy of Taylor Henson; and, despite the different types of positions into which they were hired, relations between black and white workers were cordial and often friendly. "Everybody was treated equally, all friends and buddies," Jewell Willis recalls, "and everybody was accepted, shared lunches, laughed and cursed together," even though they "left the job [heading home in] different directions."[46]

In addition to race and ethnicity, another factor that determined which types of work at the brick yard were done by whom was whether or not a given applicant was seeking permanent or temporary work. High school upperclassmen who were seeking temporary work might be hired at the brick yard or the railroad company to carry drinking water for the workers. Jewell Willis does not recall the sawmills hiring temporary workers, and thus the lumber industry was largely closed to young men seeking summer employment. Many of Malvern's African American high school boys saw their summer work in those industries that were willing to hire them as an opportunity not only to earn extra money, but to enhance their physical conditioning for the fall football season.[47] Dr. Samuel Benson, a former Malvern high school football player, remembers that a position at the brick plant was "perfect for summer's work if you were playing football in the fall." Some of the high school-aged summer employees would make a game of competing with the strongest men at the plant, many of whom, Dr. Benson recalls, "were just incredible." Some were so strong that they could "have a wheelbarrow full of brick and dance with it." Though few Malvern high school students could match the strength of the strongest permanent employees at the yards, the simple experience of working at the plant was enough to confer bragging rights to school mates who believed that moving bricks was "about as manly a thing as you [could] do, physically." At the start of the school year, young men could be overheard in the hallways, boasting to their peers, "Look, I wheeled bricks last summer."[48]

Chapter II

A School to Call Their Own: Early "Colored" Education in Malvern and Perla

"It was just a brick building, but it was a beautiful school."

—Jewell Wills, Jr., Malvern Colored
High School, Class of 1952

Public education for African Americans arrived in Malvern on the heels of a period of rapid growth in the region's black population. This increase, during the late 19th and early 20th centuries, in both the number and percentage of African American families in the area was itself a result of the expansion of the region's earliest major industries, lumber and brick. Offering opportunities for stable non-agrarian labor to black as well as white workers, the sawmills and brick yards of Malvern and Perla attracted African Americans not only from other cities in the region, but from other parts of Arkansas and surrounding states, as well. By the 1920s, the great majority of black families in Malvern and Perla had achieved job security and financial stability, and the adults in the community increasingly turned their attention to insuring even greater fortunes for their children. A cornerstone of black Malvern and Perla residents' vision for securing the future prosperity of the coming generations was the establishment of public schools, this in a state whose support for African American equality in public accommodations—from streetcars, to restrooms, to classrooms— was erratic, at best.

In 1852, Massachusetts became the first state in the U.S. to establish compulsory public education, followed shortly after by New York (in 1853). Although the Arkansas Common School Law of 1842 required municipalities to set aside a portion of the land in each township of the state for the establishment of a public school, compliance with this legislation was inconsistent. It was not until Reconstruction that public education was fully instituted, statewide. In 1866, the so-called "rebel" legislature in Arkansas established a common school system that prohibited African Americans from attending any public schools except those reserved specifically for "colored students."[49] Two years later, on the heels of the Federal Reconstruction Act of 1867, the Reconstruction General Assembly of Arkansas held a state constitutional convention at Little Rock, adopting a new legislative document that included, among other features, a provision for the education of all students, regardless of race.[50] In the same year, the General Assembly passed legislation to end segregation in Arkansas public accommodations and to impose stiff fines on those individuals and institutions that failed to offer accommodations to African Americans that were "the same and equal" to those that they offered to whites. The act imposed standards for the treatment of African Americans in public education, requiring school districts to furnish black children with facilities that were "like and equal" to those provided for white children.[51] In addition to these provisions for equal statewide primary and secondary education for all students, the period of Reconstruction, (from 1865 to 1877) saw the establishment of two colleges specifically for the education of black people. The Legislative Act of 1873 established the Branch Normal College (renamed as the University of Arkansas-Pine Bluff, in 1972), and the United Methodist Church established Philander Smith College in Little Rock in 1877.

Despite these advances, however, widespread public education for African American students was slow in coming to Arkansas. Land constraints, funding disputes, and other obstacles slowed the pace at which black schools were built, often stalling development indefinitely. In addition, after Reconstruction, segregationist Democrats in the state assembly began to work actively and openly to undermine or repeal much of the anti-racist legislation that the Reconstruction-era assembly had approved. Most notable among these segregationist Dixiecrats was Governor and former State Attorney General Jefferson "Jeff" Davis. Davis held the office of governor from 1901 to 1907, when he was elected to the U.S. Senate. As Arkansas governor, Davis supported a legislative proposal to base the funding for black public schools in Arkansas on those funds generated from black taxpayers. Fortunately, the legislation failed. Still, Davis's support for this proposal marked a turning point in the movement to bolster the cause of segregation throughout the state. Historian John William Graves notes that, "Although bills incorporating [this] proposal had been before the legislature since the 1890s, Davis was the first chief executive to support the idea."[52] Such high profile support for this racist provision, from an avowed segregationist governor, lent legitimacy and hope to those quarters of the Arkansas legislature (and the electorate) that opposed integration and racial equality.

Governor Davis's hostility to African American education and upward mobility was not shared in all regions of the state. West-central Arkansas (including Malvern, Perla, Hope, Rockport, Hot Springs, and surrounding cities) offered black students at least some limited access to primary, secondary, and even post-secondary education. Throughout the mid-1890s, the College of Hot Springs offered a normal school curriculum, designed to prepare young black men and women to serve as teachers in their communities. Though few records of this institution remain, *The Christian Recorder*, the 19th century's most influential African American weekly, published a brief report of its May 1895 commencement exercises, held in Hot Springs, at the Visitor's Chapel A.M.E. Church.[53]

In the same year, the State Superintendent of Public Instruction conducted a review of the College of Hot Springs. The final assessment, published in his biennial report, found the students in the program to be committed, hard-working, and industrious. In his formal assessment, M.R. Perry, who conducted the study of what he referred to as "Garland County's Negro Normal," reports that although the rigor of the county and state examinations led to significant attrition among the enrolled students (or what he called "quite a decrease in attendance"), "the interest in the work" by those who remained in the program "never abated." Perry's report goes on to observe that with the exception of those who left the program following the state and county exams, "[he] never saw a normal so faithfully attended or more cordially supported by both teachers and public."[54]

Perla Elementary

In 1912, Leo M. Favrot was appointed to serve as the first agent of the Negro Division of the Arkansas Department of Education. This development marked a turning point in African American education throughout the state. A Louisiana native and the son of a Confederate colonel, Favrot was in charge of overseeing improvements in African American education, and he approached his duties with great enthusiasm. One of his first undertakings in this post was to create five summer education programs—five summer normal schools—for African American teachers, a move that was praised in the pages of *The Southern Workman*, a prominent black political and educational journal of the day. The goal of this program, whose sites were distributed throughout the state, was, in Favrot's own words, "To place within the reach of the vast majority of Negro teachers in Arkansas such training as will fit them for their work."[55]

Favrot was succeeded in the Arkansas Department of Education by John A. Presson, whose is primarily remembered for his Booker T. Washington-like faith in the value of industrial training for rural southern blacks. Though he is known to have expressed wonderment that the African American professors at the state's black colleges (Shorter College, Philander Smith College, Branch Normal College, and Arkansas Baptist) preferred a liberal arts and sciences-based curriculum, he was largely unsuccessful in persuading the state's black communities to adopt his industrial training-based model; and as African American public education slowly expanded throughout Arkansas, most new primary and secondary schools privileged literature, science, and mathematics in their classroom curricula.[56]

Established in 1926, Perla Elementary School offered a curriculum that prioritized the liberal arts and sciences-based subjects favored by African American college professors and school instructors over the industrial training programs supported by the State Department of Education. Reading, writing, and mathematics were the focus at Perla Elementary. The school and its academic offerings reflected the desire of Hot Spring County's African American families to provide opportunities for their children that would prepare them for success and prosperity in a rapidly industrializing society.

Malvern Colored Elementary School

From 1926 to 1929, the teachers and parents in Malvern's black community proudly supported Perla Elementary in its mission to prepare the African American children of the region's brick workers, housekeepers, lumbermen, and small business owners to achieve even greater prosperity than their mothers and fathers, and in a wider range of careers. Teachers like Mrs. Lendora Miles and Mrs. Lois Walsh encouraged their young students to dream without limits and to pursue their most ambitious goals. Despite this encouragement, though, the black children in the area were constrained in their pursuit by the fact that Hot Spring County provided no high school program for youth of African descent. Those black students who wished to pursue a full secondary education found themselves in the predicament of having to travel far from home, most often to Little Rock, simply to continue their studies past the elementary school level.

In 1908, in a city nearly 700 miles away from the Hot Springs County seat, a series of developments was launched that would eventually expand the educational opportunities for black students in Malvern and Perla, transforming African American education in Hot Spring County and, as a result, black life in general. These events centered on a northern business-man who not only had never worked in education, but whose roots were in the textile industry. That figure was Julius Rosenwald, and in 1908 he became the president of Sears, Roebuck and Co.

Born the son of German Jewish immigrants in Springfield, Illinois, Rosenwald was sent to New York during his teenage years to train as an apprentice in the clothing business run by his mother's family. In 1885, he co-founded a menswear manufacturing company with cousin Julius Weill. This business became his entry into the Sears, Roebuck and Co. establishment, when Rosenwald and Weill began supplying men's clothing for sale through the Sears catalog division. In 1895, Rosenwald was invited to become a partner in the growing corporation. The department store thrived under Rosenwald's influence, leading the company to promote him to the presidency only 13 years later.

Rosenwald's promotion to the head of what was at the time the most profitable retail operation in the United States set him on the path that would eventually lead him to become the greatest patron of African American primary and secondary education in the history of the country. Rosenwald served as the president of Sears, Roebuck, and Co. from 1908 until

1924, when he was appointed chairman of the board, a position he held until his death. During his time at the helm of the nation's largest retail corporation, he amassed a fortune of more than $200 million dollars. He would spend the remainder of his life redistributing his wealth, through his extensive philanthropic activity in the arts, Jewish charities, and public and private primary, secondary, and post-secondary schools. Rosenwald donated generously to a number of majority white institutions across the nation, but he is best noted for his generous and unprecedented support for African American public education in the South.

In 1912, Julius Rosenwald became a trustee of Tuskegee Institute. Later that same year, impressed by the Chicago philanthropist's interest in African American education, Tuskegee founder Booker T. Washington contacted him with a request. Having established his Institute as a normal school and post-secondary training program serving black Americans in the rural inland regions of the south, Washington now wished to turn his efforts towards elementary, middle, and secondary schooling. In a private meeting, Washington approached Rosenwald about supporting his dream of greatly expanding the number of schools for African Americans in rural and small-town communities throughout the Deep South. Washington envisioned these as feeder schools for Tuskegee and other similar institutions. Subsequent historical accounts describe Rosenwald as "fascinated" by Booker T. Washington, whose goal of establishing free public schools for black children throughout the southern states was ideally suited to the retail mogul's philanthropic interests.[57] On August 12, 1912, Rosenwald celebrated his 50th birthday by making a number of generous donations, including a $25,000 gift to Tuskegee Institute. The donation funded matching grants to African American teacher training programs that followed the Tuskegee model. Washington asked Rosenwald for his permission to use the remainder to build six public schools in rural Alabama. These six, in Notasulga, Brownsville, Loachapoka, Chewacla, Big Zion, and Madison Park, were the very first Rosenwald schools.

In 1914, Rosenwald made his second major gift for the funding of African American education, releasing $30,000 for the construction of 100 rural school buildings in black communities. A larger gift, in 1916, provided seed money for the construction of an additional 200 buildings, and in 1917 the millionaire philanthropist established the Julius Rosenwald Fund in order to support and administer what had become a fully-fledged school building program. In the coming years, virtually all southern states would appoint Rosenwald agents, charged with the specific task of administering the construction of Rosenwald-funded schools in their respective jurisdictions. 1918 saw the appointment of Tuskegee graduate Percy L. Dorman as the Rosenwald building agent for the state of Arkansas.

Dorman served in this position until 1922, when he was replaced by the competent and influential R.S. Childress. Childress was the first student to earn a baccalaureate degree from Philander Smith College and only the second African American to hold a post in the Arkansas State Department of Education. Childress would remain the state's Rosenwald agent until 1932, when Julius Rosenwald died and the fund's school building program came to a close. It was in 1929, under Childress's leadership, that the Malvern Rosenwald School was built. The cost to construct the school was $18,540, and it was one of the most expensive schools to be funded by Rosenwald monies during that year. Of that amount, $200 came from the contributions of local area black residents, $16,150 was financed with public revenue, and $2,100 came from the Julius Rosenwald Fund.

Initially built to serve grades one through nine, Malvern Colored Elementary is one of only a small number of original Rosenwald structures still standing today. Erected on nine acres of land on Acme Street, on the city's west side, the school was designed in the classic bungalow style. Constructed of asphalt, concrete, and locally-made bricks, the structure is listed on the National Register of Historic Places.[58] Former students remember the school fondly and have spearheaded an effort to renovate and preserve the building for use by future generations.

Malvern Colored Elementary School was a simple brick structure, large and unembellished; but when Jewell Willis describes the building that once held Malvern's Rosenwald school, you can still detect his pride in having attended there. "It was just a brick building," he recalls," but it was a beautiful school."[59] Former student Gerald Jordan (Wilson High School, Class of 1966) remembers it as "a big huge one-room school that could be divided into three classrooms by lowering the chalkboard to [create] half size walls."[60] The school surroundings included a playground with a swing set and a carousel.[61] The building and its setting were of simple and practical design, but for the African American students who attended classes there, Malvern Colored Elementary was a magical place. Pete Willis describes it as "beautiful"; and, indeed, there was great beauty in its very existence as the first public school in Malvern created specifically to serve the educational needs and goals of the region's black boys and girls.

As in most segregated school systems of the period, Malvern Colored Elementary was less generously funded than its white counterparts. Supplies, for example, were the cast-offs and hand-me-downs no longer needed or wanted by the students and teachers at the area's majority-white schools. Jewell Willis recalls receiving boxes of crayons that were "half-used" by the students in Malvern and Perla's white elementary classes. So too were the black students' textbooks. Here Willis describes the experience of receiving second-hand textbooks at the beginning of each school year:

> Every fall [when] school started in September they would bring huge boxes of books ... I'd get about 5 or 6 boxes; and we had to go through [those boxes] to get books. A lot of them were advanced ... and so we had to dig in there [to find the appropriate level]. They wasn't separated out for us.[62]

However disadvantaged in terms of resources, Malvern Colored Elementary was rich in other areas, like the support of the African American community, the involvement of area parents, and—most notably—the skill and dedication of its teachers. At a time when teachers could be certified with only a high school diploma and one year of college (or less, in some circumstances), some of Malvern's instructors had greater than the required minimum levels of education, and in a variety of fields. "[O]ur teachers [were] knowledgeable to teach several subjects," notes Willis.[63] In addition to academic instruction, the Malvern Colored Elementary faculty also took very seriously their responsibility to provide their young charges with the structure and discipline to succeed in the classroom and beyond. Explains Alvin Murdoch, "Those teachers were really the ones that gave me and a lot of other children their foundation to move on in life."[64] Laura Hunter remembers the teachers as strict, "but never vicious."[65] Instructors and disciplinarians at school, Malvern Colored Elementary teachers also functioned as mentors and role models outside of the classroom. Explains Alvin Murdoch, "They had a lot of influence because they were our Sunday school teachers, they were our neighborhood mentors, and they really had full control of our basic education and molding our little lives."[66]

Committed to educating Malvern's black children both inside the classroom and out, Malvern Colored Elementary teachers were beloved by their students, whose recollections of their favorite instructors portray a team of committed, dynamic men and women whose skills in the classroom were matched only by their dedication and compassion. Judy Pierce remembers her favorite instructor, Mrs. Cooper, as "a great teacher."[67] One of two fourth grade instructors (the other was Lendora Miles), Mrs. Cooper covered the class for half of the day, at which point students would transfer to Mrs. Miles's room.

A teacher of both fourth and second grades, Mrs. Lendora Miles was both affectionate and stern, a combination that Alvin Murdoch describes as "grandmotherly love." The structure and discipline in her classroom was tempered by her kindness and warmth. "She would always use a hug and … a pat on the back in order to get you to where she needed you to be in her class," Murdoch recalls.[68] Mrs. Miles was as beloved for her compassion as she was respected for her keen intellect. Marva Jasper remembers Mrs. Miles as a "a brilliant lady" with "a lot of talent" and as a "great historian" who was "loved by everybody."[69] John Hill remembers Mrs. Miles as an exceedingly knowledgeable historian and poet whose mind was "just as sharp as a razor." Lillian Beard (Malvern Colored High School, Class of 1950) recalls her as "an interesting woman" who was "smart."[70] Explains Beard, "If I had any homework and I needed somebody to explain it to me, Miss Miles could do it even though she wasn't my teacher."[71]

For Laura and Jimmy Hunter, fifth grade meant spending the year under the strict but compassionate tutelage of Mrs. Allen. "She was really … tough on us," remembers Mrs. Hunter; but the emphasis on discipline in hers and other classrooms helped to create an optimal environment for learning.[72] Says Mrs. Hunter, "I don't remember fights. There was never trouble."[73] Jimmy Hunter echoes this sentiment in the following observation: "[Mrs. Allen] was probably the strictest teacher I've ever had in my entire life. She was very, very stern; but when you got out of her class you knew what you were doing."[74]

Another memorable fifth grade teacher was Miss Future Mae Harvey. John Hill (Malvern Senior High School, Class of 1969) and Alvin Murdoch, remember Miss Harvey for her ability to maintain high standards for classroom behavior and obedience while, at the same time, instilling in all of her students a deeply affecting sense of her faith in their abilities. Explains

Hill, "She was stern, but she was like a mother figure; and if you got wrong she would chastise you, but she was always there to encourage you."[75] Alvin Murdoch echoes Hill's characterization of Harvey's unique combination of discipline and encouragement in the following remembrance:

Miss Harvey was a ... stern teacher, and in her grade you'd reach your top ability. She didn't allow for any nonsense. She would always encourage you, but she always had the stature to be forceful. I had her in the fifth grade and at that time she would demand that you do your best, and she would put the pressure on you to get the best out of you. And that was my memory of Mrs. Harvey ... She would not let you fail, she would one-on-one you and reach up and have you reach back and she would always [say] "I talked to your mother and I talked to your father so I know you and I know you can do better." And she would give us that as a way to extract the best out of you.[76]

One of the most beloved instructors at Malvern Colored Elementary was Mrs. Lois Walsh. Remembered for her skill as a first grade teacher, for her high standards for student behavior and academic performance, and for her impeccable style, Mrs. Lois Walsh made a positive and lasting impression on all she encountered. "I remember my first grade teacher very well," says Judy Pierce, "Mrs. Walsh was my first grade teacher and she was so wonderful. She was just, you know, like a bright ray of sunshine."[77] Alvin Murdoch recalls "her neatness" and "her particularness." She was, he explains, "particular about how you approach[ed] your learning," and "she would always tutor you in how to start your learning process." Always willing to provide extra help to those students who needed it, Mrs. Walsh "would give you long lessons on stature and what it takes to be a good student and to look forward toward the future."[78] Known for her sophisticated style of dress and admired for her beauty, Mrs. Walsh was a natural choice as a role model for the young girls at her school. Lillian Beard remembers her as a lovely and kind woman with whom she simply enjoyed spending time. "I liked Lois Walsh," she recalls. "Every day at lunchtime I would go to Miss Walsh's room and I think it was because I thought she was pretty and she always would compliment me."[79] Laura Hunter remembers Mrs. Walsh as "an elegant lady" and a "unique person" who was "very grammatical and very correct."[80] In Mrs. Walsh's classroom, "Everything had to be correct, because she was correct" explains Judy Pierce, "and so she was a great teacher."[81]

Another beloved first grade teacher was Mrs. Nancy Ross. Jewell Willis remembers her fondly as "very caring" and as a "very, very loving teacher." Mrs. Ross was particularly skilled at helping her young students to develop school-appropriate comportment and focus. Recounts Willis, "[she] had a way to settle you down and concentrate." [82]

In addition to skilled and dedicated teachers, Malvern Colored Elementary also benefitted from the strong leadership of its principal. Mrs. Emma Lee Peyton was one of Malvern Colored Elementary School's most respected principals. Strong of character and spirit, Mrs. Peyton understood the importance of order and discipline in the classroom and in the hallways, and she was willing and ready to dole out punishments in order to aid her students in learning the importance of obedience, self-respect, and self-control. "She was very strict," recalls Jewell Willis, "and what Mrs. Peyton said, that was the law." Willis did, occasionally, find himself on the receiving end of Mrs. Peyton's corporal punishment and, thus, his recollection that "she had a good right hand for whipping" rings with an authenticity that only comes from direct experience.[83]

Principal Peyton believed in teaching by example, and when circumstances compelled her to give out punishments, she did so in such a way that all of her students were reminded of the consequences that disobedience and mischief could bring. Willis recounts the spectacle of Mrs. Peyton's spankings:

> [In] our school ... all the classrooms were parallel, and in the center of the building was an auditorium; and Mrs. Peyton had ... a straight back chair, and what she would do when she was getting ready to punish someone, especially the boys ... [is] put us in the hallway and have all of the doors open to the other classrooms ... She had what we called the *electric chair* ... and when you had cut up, you know, [when the] classroom teacher couldn't handle you ... you had to go to Mrs. Peyton, and Mrs. Peyton would set you in the chair and twist about two of three of those switches together ... And what she would do, you would have to sit in that chair and she'd take about three paces back, and she would come across your legs.[84]

27

Though Willis does not consider Mrs. Peyton's punishments to be excessive or harsh, he does believe they were an effective deterrent against excessive mischief and tomfoolery. "She didn't kill nobody," he recalls, "but you walked a straight line."[85]

Perhaps the most memorable principal of Malvern Colored Elementary was Mrs. Sophronia Tuggle. Revered as a leader and visionary whose high standards for the performance of both her teachers and her students helped strengthen African American public education at all levels, she is also remembered as Malvern Colored Elementary's final authority on school rules and discipline. Laura Hunter remembers that "if you didn't hear the bell when the bell rang, you were in trouble." She recalls one incident in particular, when she was "just having a lot of fun on the playground," and she didn't hear the bell. A young girl at the time, Hunter received a spanking for her tardiness. Hunter "didn't like to get spanked," and she remembers the punishment to this day.[86]

In Malvern's African American community, teachers and parents were allies in the effort to cultivate disciplined, well-educated, and responsible young men and women, and each student's family took on the duty of reinforcing the lessons learned in Malvern Colored Elementary School classrooms. Families were informed whenever students were punished, through notes indicating both the severity of the penalty and the cause. For Jewell Willis, the strict discipline practiced by the Malvern Colored Elementary principals was indicative of a broader emphasis on discipline throughout the area's black public schools. He explains, "there was no discipline problem at all at our school, and they wanted us to learn. That was the main. But to learn, you have to have discipline—not so much that we feared the teacher, but we knew that if we didn't do what the teacher said, then going home was awful, you know, with a note."[87]

Chapter III

From Leopard Power to Dragon Pride: Malvern's "Colored" High Schools

"When you're growing up around here, that was one of the most important things that a young man would want to do here in Malvern, is play football."

—Charlie Carroll, Malvern Colored
High School, Class of 1952

Oh Wilson Dear, We will keep near
The things that thou has taught,
And as we travel on life's way
Remember joys thou brought.

Let's give three cheers for Wilson High
And never let her die.
We'll stand by thee, Dear Wilson High
And praise thee to the sky.
—Wilson High School alma mater

Malvern Colored High School (1944-1952)

During its first 13 years, the academic program at Malvern Colored Elementary school extended only from the first through ninth grades. In 1943, however, in response to black citizen demands, the Hot Spring County School Board expanded the curriculum at the school to include the 10th grade. In 1943, the school board added 11th grade, and in 1944, the board added a 12th and final grade to the Malvern Colored School curriculum. For the first time in its history, the city's African American students were given the same opportunity to earn a high school diploma as their white counterparts.

If the school board decisions of 1942, 1943, and 1944 paved the way for historic change in the prospects for African American students in Hot Spring County, then 1945 brought the promise of these developments to fruition. In that year, Malvern Colored Elementary was renamed Malvern Colored Elementary and High School and Mr. A. Tate was appointed to serve as its principal. Thus, in a year that saw the end of World War II, the death of President Franklin Delano Roosevelt, and the creation of the United Nations, Malvern Colored High School graduated its first seven high school seniors. They were: Leon Wilson, Zelma Scott, Val Wright, Albert Fanning, Jemmy V. Hawkins, Clovis Wright, and Tecola Lee.

Many of the teachers and administrators at Malvern Colored High School were long-established educators who had begun their careers at Malvern Colored Elementary, Perla Elementary, or at the black elementary school in neighboring Rockport. Jewel Willis remembers Mrs. Henrietta Bailey as "strict…, but also a loving and caring teacher."[88] Mrs. Bailey was his favorite teacher, and one memory of her exemplifies the combination of structure, discipline, and compassion that she brought to the classroom experience. Willis shares this anecdote:

> I will never forget [when] she told us back in…'48, '49, she said, "All right, you have to study and get your lesson. One day there won't be any pick and shovels or broom." And we [students] just couldn't get the concept in our minds. We said, "Well, okay, there's going to always be pick and shovels." But [today], you've got machinery and a lot of the … factories and plants [have] electric and gas sweepers.[89]

In moments like the one Jewel Willis describes, Mrs. Bailey tried to build in her students an awareness of the importance of academic readiness, and she made herself available to students for individualized and small-group tutoring and mentoring in order to prepare them for the rapidly changing employment landscape of the mid-20th-century South. Recalls Willis, "[S]he was fair, she taught us well, and you could stay after [for extra help] for hours."[90]

Among the most salient memories of the Malvern Colored High School alumni are those of their principals. Principal Horace Jones, Principal Edward Bailey, Principal Ethel Beckly, and Principal A. Tate are uniformly described as firm disciplinarians who were as committed to their students' moral and character development as they were to their academic growth. Second only to the respect and admiration with which Malvern Colored High School alumni recall their teachers and principals is the passion and pride with which they remember their high school football team, the Malvern Colored High School Leopards.

One of the most important rites of passage for many of Malvern's young African American men was participation on the high school football team. The physicality of the sport, the discipline of practice, and the necessity of working as a team taught invaluable lessons in persistence, hard work, and conflict management. Dr. Samuel Benson remembers that there was "kind of a community expectation that you would grow up, and at about 12 or 13 you would get a chance to play football on the Malvern Colored High School football team."[91] For Dr. Benson, football provided a first-hand lesson in toughness and endurance, and he remembers his gradual progress from timid football novice to experienced veteran player:

> I started at 12 and I think I cried every day when I was 12 years old. They used to beat me up bad. It didn't hurt me but just roughed me up. Thirteen I cried very little, but by the time I was 14, man, you had something to deal with. And, of course, at 15 and 16 I was starting and I made All-State and stuff like that. But that was [something I] had to overcome. I mean, I was 12. Some people were playing when they're 20, so you know how they threw me around; but a couple of years later it was an altogether different thing. It really changed.[92]

Malvern Colored High School offered limited sporting options for its students. "During this time ... in our athletic department, we didn't have track," Jewell Willis recalls. "[W]e had a basketball team. We didn't have baseball, but we had sandlot baseball ... after school, but this wasn't a curricular activity."[93] Willis began playing for the Leopards football squad when he was a freshman or sophomore in high school and, for him, the physical challenge of being a rookie on the team amounted to a simple issue of size and weight. "That first year," he recalls, "you weighed 125 pounds or something like that, and these other guys are 160 and 170 pounds"; and yet, despite the weight difference, the older, bigger players had "no mercy."[94]

Of the various sports offered at the school, football received the most generous allotment of the school's limited sports budget; and of the portion that remained after the football team was funded, the greater share went to boys' sports. "[The girls] had basketball," recalls Willis, "but there was no track, no volleyball curriculum for the girls." "With the finances in the male department," he explains, "we pretty well got what we wanted [but] the girls, they got just a little bit." For this reason as well as because of the large number of boys and girls who participated—if not as players, then as cheerleaders, band members, majorettes, and spectators—football was the most popular extra-curricular activity at the school.

To say that Malvern Colored High School football received the lion's share of the sports budget at the school should not be construed as confirmation that the team was well-funded. Jewell Willis's description of the dual role of the Leopards football coaches highlights the vast difference between the resources available to the Malvern Colored High School team and the monies allotted to high school football teams today, in the 21st century. "During this time," explains Willis, "the coaches ... didn't have what they've got now ... and so, during my years, they was classroom teachers and also coaches"; and he contrasts the role of the instructor/athletic coaches of his youth with the larger, more specialized coaching staffs for today's high school teams: "Every position now, you've got coaches to coach that position."[95]

Underfunded not only by today's standards but also in comparison with the white high school football teams in the area, Malvern Colored High School football was, nonetheless, adept at extracting the maximum benefit from the limited financial support it received from both public and private sources. Regional convention dictated that, in school districts that maintained both black and white high schools, the football team at the African American school be allotted a lower operating budget than its white counterpart. "In other words," explains Jewell Willis, "if [the school district] had a budget of $10,000, the white school got $8,000 and the black school got maybe $2,000." For members of Malvern's black high school football team, this meant that many of its supplies were handed down when they were no longer needed or desired by the team at the all-white Malvern Senior High School. Just as the students in Malvern's African American classrooms had access only to the worn and discarded textbooks from the city's white schools, so too did the black students who played on the school's sports teams depend on the second-hand uniforms passed down by their district's white players. Jewell Willis remembers receiving a batch of used shoulder pads "that was half tore."[96] Used football shoes often posed the greatest challenge for Malvern's black football players. Lillian Beard remembers hearing from her husband, who was the Malvern Colored High School football captain during the 1946 season, that he sometimes had to play with two left shoes.[97] Jewell Willis remembers the difficult situation that arose when the team happened to recruit two players who wore size 12 shoes, unusual for high school-aged boys of that era. The football team from the white school had only passed on one pair of size 12 shoes, and so, recounts Willis, "One would take one for his left foot" while his teammate would take the right shoe, and each would put "his street shoes or tennis shoes" on the other foot.[98]

Jerseys were improvised. Jewell Willis describes how the teams created uniforms using the most affordable materials available: "We didn't have jerseys, we had sweatshirts. [Do] you remember the shoe polish that had the little adapter in it? We would have to take the shoe polish and put a number on there. That was the jerseys." Nor were the jerseys provided by the school district. "Your parents had to buy your sweatshirt if you were going to play," recalls Willis, "because the school ... didn't have enough money to do that."[99] By the time he had begun playing football, his school was able to afford helmets for all of its players.[100] A few years earlier, though, when Lillian Beard's husband was playing, the school district provided no helmets for Malvern's black players. Referring to the willingness of her husband and his teammates to play without protective head gear, Lillian Beard jokes that, "they didn't even know what a helmet was, but they played football and they enjoyed it because they didn't know any better. They hadn't been exposed to what they were supposed to have; they were exposed to what [the school district] gave them."[101]

Eventually, the Malvern Colored High School team did receive its own custom uniforms. "We got new uniforms in 1949," recalls Jewell Willis. "Our colors were blue and gold. Oh, we was proud. We were proud just like we had a tuxedo, you know?" He still remembers his number (24) and that of his teammate, Charlie Carroll (20).

In its earliest years, in the mid-1940s, Malvern's black high school football team often found itself at a disadvantage against the teams fielded by schools from larger communities like Pine Bluff, Little Rock, and Hope. During its earliest days, the Malvern Colored High School football team suffered several painful defeats. Jewell Willis recalls a particularly stinging loss to Texarkana. The game, which he remembers as "pretty sloppy," ended in a 77-0 win for the opposition. By the end of the 1940s, though, the Leopards had achieved a stunning reversal of fortune on the playing field, most of it taking place in the half year that separated the 1948 football season from the 1949 season. Willis recounts the Leopard's dramatic rise from struggling small-town squad to a regional football power:

> We won our first championship in 1949, and ... in 1948 we didn't win a game. [We] scored one touchdown the whole year ... Then we came back with dedication and hard work and we won the championship the next year. So that goes to show you what kind of improvement we had, and we were very proud of it.[102]

The team won additional championships in 1950 and 1951.

Much of the success of the Malvern Colored High School Leopards was due to the committed leadership and mentoring provided by coaches like S.E. Bullock and Vernon Norman, the latter of whom was both a bandleader and the Leopards' football coach during the 1951-52 school year. Former Leopard football player Jewell Willis attributes the winning season of 1949 primarily to Bullock, who stepped into the position of football coach some time prior to the fall of 1948. Bullock's first year saw little in the way of on-field success for the team, but the year of conditioning and practice would pay off in the coming season. "We didn't win a game," recalls Willis, "but he got us on the right track, [and] in 1949 we won the championship; and then we were off all the way up to 3 more years of championship teams."[103]

Jewell Willis remembers Coach Bullock as, "a very strict and demanding man." Described as a "large man" and "a physical man," Bullock's great size and physical nature deeply influenced both his style of coaching and the type of football he expected his team members to play. "He expected us to be mentally and physically tough," recalls Willis, and Coach Bullock ran his practices accordingly. Willis remembers that, "We had to practice as though we were in a game, and some of our practices—you can ask [teammates] Dr. Samuel Benson and Charlie Carroll—was rougher than it was when we played a game."[104] The coach was a stickler for conditioning, and he used his legendary paddle as a very compelling motivation for his young charges to push themselves to the peak of their abilities. Willis explains a typical practice:

[H]e would do a lot on our physical activity. He would put us all in one straight line. And he had an old paddle board, and he would start us from the south part of the campus and make us run all the way down to the school; and he would be in the middle, and what he would do, when he blew the whistle for us to start running the sprints [is] he would have that paddle and whoever was kind of lagging behind, that's who he would paddle. Now, it was not as bad as it seems, because when you got on pads and he hit you with his paddle, you know, it sounded like a shotgun [which was] more a mental thing than it was … physical.[105]

Though these conditioning methods can appear harsh and even cruel in the current era of no-score youth soccer leagues, Coach Bullocks' athletes adored and respected him not in spite of but because of his rigorous and exacting coaching standards and techniques. "We had to do a whole lot of sweat and tears," recalls Willis. "He demanded [and] got the best out of you [and] we loved the guy, we loved the man."[106]

The success of the Malvern Colored High School football team may have contributed to the school district's eventual decision to withdraw some of its support from the program. During the mid-1940s, Malvern's white high school permitted the black football team to hold games in its stadium, a privilege that was revoked in the late 1940s. Some former players have speculated that there may have been a link between the black team's rise as a regional power and the white high school's decision to close its stadium to the Malvern Colored Leopards and their fans. Jewell Willis is among those who have long believed in a connection between the two developments. He explains:

> The white team, they had a stadium. They would allow the black to play in that stadium; but we became so powerful and so good that they decided that ... we would have to get our own stadium to play in because the focus was off of the white boys ... we had a turnout from all of the community. And, not only that—when we traveled, our parents and uncles and cousins and friends, they would load up the car and they would travel with us to see us play. We had it going on [and] we were good.[107]

Community support for the Malvern Colored High School Leopards was quite strong, and the team could count among its fans black spectators as well as white. Willis explains:

> Definitely we had the support of the community, because whenever we played, basically the whole community would turn out. People that didn't know anything too much about football, the rules and regulations, they would come to see us play. I mean the white and colored.[108]

Mrs. Frances Calhoun was among the team's most dedicated supporters, and her son, Dr. Samuel Benson, fondly recalls her commitment to the team throughout his years on the Leopard football squad: "[M]y mother went to every one of my football games ... Every football game I played, [she] was always there, no matter how far away it was. [She] always drove to see me play."[109]

Among those organizations whose presence added to the spectacle and pageantry of the Leopards football games were the Malvern Colored High School Cheerleaders, the Malvern Colored High School Band, and the Malvern Colored High School Majorettes. The cheerleading squad, the pep squad, and the majorettes were activities open only to girls, while the band was open to both girls and boys, alike. Lillian Beard was in the very first band organized at the high school, and her participation offered her an opportunity to further hone the musical skills that she was already utilizing as an instrumentalist for her church. Among the boys who were active in the band were Jim Moore and Billy Earl Jones, who served during the late 1940s as the Drum Major and Second Drum Major, respectively. It was not until 1940 that Malvern Colored High School had its first squad of majorettes. The Malvern Colored High School Majorettes were founded by student Mary Bell Bryant, who formed her organization with the support of then Principal Edward Bailey. The first four women to serve as majorettes for the school were Baby Ruth Morgan, Hannah Jean Merriweather, Orrie Lee Merriweather and, of course, Mary Bell Bryant.[110]

A.A. Wilson High School (1952-1968)

In 1951, the Malvern School Board allotted monies and land for the construction of a new high school for African American students and, in 1952, A.A. Wilson High School opened its doors. Located at 404 North Banks Street, just south of Young Street, the school was named for Annie Agnes Wilson, a beloved and well-respected educator in Malvern's African American school system.[111] Alvin Murdoch is among the many alumni who still refer to A.A. Wilson as "Aunt Agnes Wilson High School," an indication of the deep affection that the community felt for this long-term member of Malvern's educational community. Mr. Edward Bailey was selected to serve as Wilson's principal, and he held this post until desegregation, in 1968.

The opening of A.A. Wilson high school set in motion a series of changes that resulted in the repurposing and renaming of the building that had for the previous eight years housed both Malvern Colored Elementary and Malvern Colored High School. Once the African American secondary programs moved to the new A.A. Wilson building, the older Rosenwald building was reappointed the Malvern Colored Elementary School, and in 1953, long-term Malvern schoolteacher Mrs. Sophronia Tuggle was promoted to serve as its principal. In 1960, the superintendent, the school board, and the citizens of Malvern elected to rename Malvern Colored Elementary in honor of Principal Tuggle. That this was the second African American school in the city to be named after one of its respected women educators set Malvern apart from many other communities in the region.

It is notable that, at a time when many African American communities were naming their schools after prominent U.S. black historical figures like Frederick Douglass, Booker T. Washington, and Paul Laurence Dunbar, the African American community of Malvern chose to honor its teachers and principals. This speaks to the high regard in which Malvern's black community held—and continues to hold—its teachers and its schools.

In 1965, Mr. X.L. Jones was appointed the principal of Tuggle elementary, and he went on to serve in that post until desegregation, in 1968. Both Sophronia Tuggle and X.L. Jones were legendary in their roles, and Malvern alumni speak their names with a mixture of hushed reverence and warm affection. After their principals, many former students' most cherished memories of Tuggle are of the friendships they made there. Gerald Jordan attended Tuggle in the sixth grade and remembers it as the place where he, as a newcomer, "met kids from other parts of town." He developed close relationships with "Rodney English and Ronnie Jones and Ronald Morgan and Billy Earl Blackman, Ace Lock and then all the folks who later became classmates and friends for a long, long time."[112] For Samuel Bryant, his memories of Tuggle are primarily of his instructors, including first grade teacher Miss Ora Lee Cook, the "vivid" and "demanding" second grade teacher Miss Taylor, and third grade teacher Miss Cotter.[113]

Sixth grade marked a milestone in the academic lives of Malvern's African American students. Alvin Murdoch explains: "In those days, high school started in the seventh grade. Wilson was the high school, so from the sixth grade we had a little graduation which was a big event, and then ... we went to high school."[114] Judy Pierce remembers the pride that she felt as a seventh grader entering Wilson High School. "[W]hen we went to school we were so happy, you know, because we were getting a chance to go to the big school," she explains. "I thought I was going to be, you know, real grown up because I was going to the A.A Wilson High School."[115] For Pierce, a new school and larger school meant new activities. "In the Tuggle Elementary School, all we did was play and get our lesson," Pierce recalls, "but in the big school, I was looking forward to being a majorette, and all those good things. I knew that once I went to the Wilson High School ... we would get a chance to do things other than play."[116] Samuel Bryant reports similar feelings of progress and maturity upon matriculating at Wilson, in his case, after completing the academic program at nearby Rockport Elementary. "After elevating from [Rockport Elementary] and then going up the hill to Wilson at the 7th grade, now that was an experience," he recalls, "because now, in the 7th grade, you're actually in the same school with seniors."[117]

Many students experienced both excitement and apprehension around the experience of sharing a school building with much older boys and girls. Alvin Murdoch explains:

> You go to high school and all those kids were seniors, juniors, sophomores and freshman, so it was a change from the nurturing elementary school to go to Aunt Agnes Wilson High School. It was a challenge and a great change from elementary to being a seventh grader in a school with seniors.[118]

A.A. Wilson aided students in negotiating the transition from being in the oldest class at their elementary school to the youngest class at the high school by creating a specific meeting place just for seventh graders. "In the seventh grade ... you didn't mingle with the twelfth graders" explains Murdoch. "They had an area for the seventh graders to be in, so you still had your bond there."[119]

Among the biggest changes for Wilson alumna Laura Hunter (A.A. Wilson High School, Class of 1964), were those regarding the school dress code. "[W]e could not wear pants at all," she remembers, "no shorts, no pants, [and] we always had to wear a dress or a skirt." Consequently, preparation for the school day included maintaining the required clothing items for her and her sisters. "In those days," she explains, "we hard pressed our clothes ... and, of course, I had to iron my two sisters' clothes, too."[120] The added labor of ironing her school clothes did not, however, detract from the excitement of finally being an A.A. Wilson student. "[A]s far as going to school," she recalls, "it was just exciting to me." She "loved going to school," and she relished new experiences like, "being able to catch the bus [to] go there." Even the experience of physical education class, with its gym suits and locker rooms, had the gratifying feel of maturity, when compared to the more free-form recess periods at Tuggle. Explains Hunter, "In those days, we had ... P.E. uniforms, and we had a chance to change into those uniforms and take a shower and change out and that was all new with me and that was fun."[121]

With its busy corridors, extracurricular activities, and more challenging coursework, A.A. Wilson High School marked the pinnacle of public education for black students, not only in the neighboring communities of Malvern and Perla, but throughout Hot Spring County. Notably, the specter of segregation and inequality did not cast a long shadow over the region's effort to educate its African American children. As in the case of its predecessor, Malvern Colored High School, the most blatant reminder of the Jim Crow realities of the time was the vast divide between the resources allocated for the textbooks and supplies at the all-white Malvern Senior High School and those set aside to purchase books and materials for A.A. Wilson students. Recalls Laura Hunter, "We had to pay fees for our books, and these were old outdated textbooks, you know … we had to pay fees to get more textbooks."[122]

Despite the disparities in funding, the black students at A.A. Wilson were no less devoted to their institution than their white counterparts were to senior high school across town. When the city's black secondary education program moved from Malvern Colored High School to A.A. Wilson, the latter school adopted a new mascot, the Dragons. When describing the meaning of the Wilson Dragons mascot in their lives as students, the word that comes to the lips of so many Wilson alumni is *pride*. "[I]t was just a great time of great pride, great school days [and], remembering back now, it was just a real great time of just having something of your own and loving it," explains Rev. Henry Mitchell (Malvern Senior High School, Class of 1972).[123] Despite segregation, the graduates of A.A. Wilson High School, like the graduates of Malvern Colored High School before them, experienced the existence of a high school program expressly for the education of black students as a privilege, the privilege of having an institution to call their own. "We didn't know that we were oppressed," recalls Rev. Mitchell. "We had everything we thought we needed and we worked with it, and it was good."[124]

Community pride in the Wilson Dragons name was only reinforced by the pageantry and spectacle of the high school's football Saturdays. Students, their, families, and even non-affiliated communities took great pleasure not only in following the fortunes of the high school football team, but in the musical offerings of the Wilson High School band and the spirited routines of the Wilson cheerleaders. For Judy Pierce, "being a Wilson Dragon was one of the best things that could have happened to a young girl," and every part of a Wilson football game was magical to her. For Pierce, "The cheers and the music and, you know, the boys playing football, I mean, all of that together, it was like a dream come true."[125]

The two greatest attractions at the high school were the Wilson Dragons football team and the Wilson High School Band. "Everybody wanted to be in ... the band," recalls Samuel Bryant, "because the band was just outstanding."[126] For some spectators, the band's half-time performance rivaled the play on the field as a point of interest. Mr. Bryant notes that, "Some people didn't even come to watch the football game; they came to watch the band because it was just incredible." In fact, the band was so outstanding and such an important phenomenon in Malvern's African American community that some have likened it to the marching bands at historically black colleges and universities. "People now think of University of Arkansas Pine Bluff (UAPB) and Grambling's band," explains Bryant, but "Wilson's bands were that awesome."

The most unique feature of the Wilson band was its ability to create spectacular performances using very few resources. Laura Hunter, who joined the band during her ninth grade year, remembers how, in its earliest years, the band depended on discarded uniforms and instruments from Malvern Senior High:

> [We got] uniforms that were worn out and we could get some of the cast off uniforms sometimes from the other school. We wore those until we could not wear those but then finally did buy some uniforms. We used old instruments—cast off instruments—but we played them, and I guess it might have been a good thing because we learned how to make those instruments work.[127]

"The band was small," recalls Hunter, who estimates that "The band might have been about twenty," including, "one drummer, one snare drummer, and one bass drummer; and we had the ... other instruments—saxophone, clarinet, flute, and trombone." Despite its small size, however, the band was able to create impressive half-time performances. "Somehow," explains Hunter, "the band director could make formations with just the few of us, and so we learned how to do that and we did perform during half time."[128]

In addition to playing at football games, the band also played in the homecoming and Christmas parades. The parades drew even larger audiences than some of the football games, attracting not only Malvern and Perla residents, but also residents from the surrounding communities. Recalls John Hill, "[P]eople would come from around, you know, just to see the band march."[129] "The people just lined up to see us," remembers Hunter. With its majorettes and both "male drum majors and female drum majors," the parades were what Hunter calls, "a sight to see." Former Wilson student Rev. Henry Mitchell remembers the band for its interpretations of 1950s and '60s hit songs.[130] Laura Hunter, on the other hand, cherishes her memories of the more traditional selections in their repertoire. She explains: "What I liked about the music in those days was that we played marches. We played John Phillip Souza and marches like that."[131] She would love to see today's marching bands turn their attention back to these beloved classics. Says Hunter, "[W]e played what I call really sound … curricula of music, and it was really nice."[132]

Despite the reign of Jim Crow throughout much of Arkansas, Malvern's parades and their audiences were somewhat integrated. While the black and white high school bands were as segregated as the institutions they represented, Laura Hunter remembers some cross-racial participation on the parade floats, as in this recollection:

> I have a memory of when I was in, maybe, kindergarten or first grade. I was a doll … I don't remember who came up with this, but there was a truck and there was a white doll and then a black doll and another white doll on one side, and the same thing on the other side. And, that far back, I can't imagine but it actually did happen, and you know, I had a little pinafore and … my cheeks were rouged and … it was the most amazing thing back then.[133]

This account underscores the cordial relations between white and African American residents of Malvern and Perla, relative to other regions of the south, and despite the cities' adherence to the statewide laws requiring segregation in public facilities.

John Hill was a member of the Wilson Dragons football team, but his memories of watching the A.A. Wilson band at the annual Christmas parade precede his football career by many years, and the sight of that organization playing its upbeat marches and making its way through the town created a lasting impression in his young mind. The Wilson High Band was the finale of the Christmas parade, and Hill can still describe the excitement of watching its members making their way through the streets:

> And ... when you heard the band coming down the highway, it was just electrifying—just chills up and down your body to see them and the way they marched ... I can't describe it in words, the feelings that we felt when the Wilson band would march.[134]

Hill remembers the Wilson band as the most popular element of both the Christmas and homecoming parades, and its loss meant the end of a beloved institution. "[W]hen Wilson dropped out of the parade because of the integration, parades haven't ... had as much punch," he explains. "[I]t was like a legacy that just died off."[135]

In its earliest years, the A.A. Wilson Marching Band wore "black and white, black pants and a white shirt and black shoes," and Laura Hunter can still recall the day when band members received their first new uniforms, as well as the series of events that led up to their purchase:

> [W]hen we was in the band, my grandmother and the band boosters—and she was one of the band boosters—they raised money. They would sell things—cookies, cakes—[and] they raised money to buy the uniforms. That's how they got uniforms then.[136]

The uniforms were, "royal blue, trimmed in gold," to match the school colors.[137] And while the band boosters were effective at raising money to cover a portion of the organization's expenses, other costs of band membership had to be shouldered by the members themselves. Laura Hunter recalls that, "In order to travel with the band you had to have 50 cents." She was fortunate in that both her immediate and extended family members were willing to pay for her participation in the Wilson band's out-of-town events. "If my parents didn't have it, my grandparents did, [and] that's how I got a chance to go on the trips," she explains, noting that, "if you didn't have the 50 cents, you could not go."[138]

The band was only one component in the pageantry of Wilson High School's music and sporting events. Cheerleaders and majorettes were also an important part of every football game and parade. When she was in ninth grade, Judy Pierce joined both the A.A. Wilson cheerleader and majorette squads. For her, membership in these groups was affirmation that she was "a real big girl," and no longer a child. "[W]e would cheer," she recalls, and "then we would dance, you know, [and] we would just have a good time," all to the music of the A.A. Wilson Band. For Pierce, cheerleading and participation as a majorette provided a rare opportunity to perform choreographed dances for a large audience. "I always loved to dance," she explains, "and when I got a chance to be a cheerleader and a majorette, I mean throwing those legs up in the air, that was all right with me."[139]

For many students, their years at A.A. Wilson were shaped by their participation on the cheerleading squad, in the band, or as a majorette. Others still found their true passion on the football playing field. For Rev. Henry Mitchell, his greatest dream was to become a Wilson football player. He "wanted to play football for the Dragons," because, for him and many other young men in the community, "The blue and gold was … better than the Los Angeles Rams."[140] For John Hill, who was all-district guard for two of his three years on the team, "playing Wilson football was a life-changing experience."[141] More than just teammates or friends, Hill's fellow players were "a family," and playing on the Dragons football squad taught him lessons about hard work and strength of character that he remembers to this day. Playing under Wilson's coaches taught him "how to succeed, how to be tough, how to go through [life]." One of Hill's most important lessons was that he did not have to be defined by other people's assumptions about his abilities. "You know," he explains, "we were taught [that] to be tough you don't have to be what they say you are."[142]

While former Dragons football payers reminisce about the camaraderie and life lessons they gained through their participation on the team, their fans recall the thrill of watching and supporting the hometown squad. For Alvin Murdoch, "The memories are great," and "the football team, the band, it was all exciting." The opening was his favorite part of the game, "watching especially the seniors, as they march[ed] on the field."[143] For Murdoch and others, Dragons football was a wonderful part of the Wilson experience. Cheerleader Judy Pierce enjoyed having close proximity to the players. During her high school years, one of her greatest pleasures was escorting the team out of the stadium, after the games. "As a cheerleader, we got a chance to walk the guys off the field," she recalls."Even though they went with their other girlfriends, we got a chance to walk them off the field, and that was a joy because you [were] just tickle pink."[144] She would eventually go on to marry a Dragons football player.

Even after Wilson was dissolved and its students were transferred to the previously all-white Malvern Senior High School, many of the Dragons football players remained closely connected, but in a very different way. In consultation with each other, a number of former Dragons decided not to play for the new coach and his team. John Hill explains:

[W]e all got together and decided we weren't going to play, you know, and those that did play, for long periods of time we didn't consider them as Dragons ... [W]e were die hard Dragons [and] all of us [were] going down together.[145]

The decision by key members of the Dragons football squad not to play at Malvern Senior High School was the basis for considerable friction between those former Wilson students who joined the Malvern Senior High team and those who did not. The tensions did not last, however, and today those who were playing Dragons football at the time of integration have a very different perspective on the events of that period. John Hill was among those Dragons players who felt betrayed by those former teammates who went on to play at Malvern Senior High; but, says Hill, "I don't feel that way now." He attributes much of the angst and resentment of the time to the passion of youth and to the challenge of leaving behind a school and a football squad that he and his teammates truly cherished. "[A]t that point in time," explains Hill, "so much was going on and ... I guess we didn't have time to react and think about it." In the end, says Hill, "We were too young, you know, [and] kids are going to think like kids."[146]

Today, more than forty years after the integration of Malvern schools brought about the closing of A.A. Wilson, former Dragons maintain a close bond. Says Hill, "regardless of where we go, when we meet, we're all football players and come together and talk."[147] At Malvern-Wilson reunions, former football players from both Malvern Colored and A.A. Wilson seek out their teammates to catch up and reminisce. John Hill recounts a humorous anecdote from the first Malvern-Wilson reunion:

[My] wife, when I first married her, we had a class reunion. Actually, it was the first class reunion we had; and that was the whole talk of the reunion—who did what, who did that, who made this—and I'll never forget [when] she told me, "If I hear one more story about the Dragons, I am going to leave."[148]

As much as Wilson alumni cherish their memories of the Dragons football team, the high school band, the majorettes, and the cheerleading squad, their fondest memories are of the teachers. For A.A. Wilson students, the teachers provided more than academic instruction. They were mentors in both academic and personal matters, imparting to students the value of hard work, modeling character and erudition, encouraging students to aspire to greatness, and providing them with the tools to achieve their most ambitious goals and dreams. For Samuel Bryant, teachers were "an extension of your own family," whose presence in both the classroom and the community insured that the values and ideals they instilled in the classroom permeated every aspect of their students' lives. Bryant remembers that,

> Most of the time the teachers ... were actually sitting in the front of the class. You would see those same teachers at church; so if you did something in school that you didn't have any business doing, they would just relay the message [to your parents] ... and then you had a double whammy, because you had to deal with the instructor and now you got to deal with mom and dad. You know the expression, "it takes a village to raise a child?" Well, that's what they did.[149]

A critical part of the education that students like Samuel Bryant received at Wilson was rooted in their instructors' teaching style. Beginning "around the 10th grade," Samuel Bryant and other Wilson students were exposed to "more of a lecture type [of instruction], getting you ready to take notes." As a result, recalls Bryant, when he and his classmates "first hit college," and courses that were "all about note-taking" and "teachers standing up lecturing, we were already prepared for that." He recalls that, "When the bulk of our class ... graduated [from Wilson] in '68, we pretty much hit the ground running when we got to college." Bryant estimates that roughly half of his class went to nearby Henderson State College (in

Arkadelphia) and, "Everybody [who] started at Henderson ... walked out of there with a degree." [150] By providing students with the preparation necessary to transition seamlessly to college-level work, Wilson teachers, like Malvern Colored High School teachers before them, insured that each group of students with whom they worked would have a wider range of opportunities and achieve even greater personal and economic success than in previous generations.

Students who attended A.A. Wilson in the 1960s encountered a younger cadre of teachers than they had ever experienced at Malvern Colored Elementary School. While many of his instructors at Wilson were more experienced veteran teachers, Alvin Murdoch recalls that several of them had only recently completed their own educations. "At the elementary school you had the mature teachers," he explains, "in their '40s, probably, and '30s; but, at Wilson you would have teachers that just came out of college so they were ... 25, 26, 27." For Murdoch, "it was exciting" to have young teachers on the faculty because, having attended college in the 1960s, they brought "a different look" and "a different feel" to the classroom environment. [151]

While Wilson alumni like Murdoch enjoyed the energy and enthusiasm of their youngest instructors, when asked to list their favorite teachers, they name both recent graduates and seasoned veterans; nor are those most influential and beloved figures on campus limited to the faculty. When asked to identify those instructors and mentors who were most dear to them, graduates recall not only teachers, but administrators, coaches, and staff. First among those memorable and influential administrators was Mr. Edward E. Bailey, Sr. who served as principal for all 14 years that A.A. Wilson High School was in operation. Rev. Henry Mitchell remembers him as "kind of strict," but "fair." After Wilson was dissolved, he was appointed to the position of Vice Principal at the newly-integrated Malvern High School.

Among the most beloved teachers at both Malvern Colored and A.A. Wilson High Schools was Mrs. Henrietta Bailey. For Wilson alumnus Gerald Jordan, her support and mentorship was transformative. As a high school student, Jordan had a strong interest in writing about sports, but it was only after sharing this interest with Mrs. Bailey that he was able to make the connection between his passion for writing and the possibility of a career in journalism. For Jordan, who would go on to a distinguished career in that field, this prompted a life-changing realization. Jordan des-cribes this moment in the following recollection:

> She [Mrs. Bailey] said, "Well, you've been writing these sports sto-ries for years. Why don't you major in journalism?" And it was like, are you kidding me? You can make a living doing this? ... I'd read Doc Young and guys in newspapers from around the country, and these were just little bits of my life that were scattered everywhere, but they were so disparate that they didn't come together in one picture until some-body made me slap my forehead and go, "wow, why not?"[152]

Jimmy Hunter remembers Mrs. Bailey as "the very best teacher that I have ever had in my life," and he takes great pride in the fact that "she was from right here at Malvern." For Hunter, Mrs. Bailey's teaching even outshined that of his college professors; and the level of accountability that she demanded from her students was a significant part of her effectiveness. "If you slacked off—if you were, say, an honor roll student and you slacked off," he explains, "you didn't have to worry about your parents getting on you. Henrietta Bailey ... knew you had the capability to do better, and she was on you like white on rice."[153]

Another teacher who made a significant impact on Wilson graduates was Mrs. Joan Henry. The wife of Coach Henry of the Dragons football team, she was one of the most respected and appreciated instructors at the school.[154] Samuel Bryant remembers her as the instructor who taught him "how to use words, when to use words, [to] know the meaning of words," who "made you love to read," and who "introduced us to literature where we could kind of give our own perception of what we read." Her emphasis on literary interpretation prepared him well for the type of coursework he would encounter in college, and he admits that he "didn't know how good Miss Henry was," until he was a freshman at Henderson State College. On his first examination as a college student, he not only earned an A on his very first test, but he also answered every question correctly. On the second test, he made another A, which prompted this encounter with his English professor:

> [On] the second test I had made an A again ... So, by now, Miss Freeman, who was my freshman English teacher, asked me to stand and

asked me what school did I graduate from. And I said I graduated from Wilson High in Malvern. She said, "[O]h, you didn't graduate from Malvern High? [He replied] "No, ma'am" ... And she said, "Who was your teacher there?" And I said, "Joan Henry." And her response was, "I see why [you've done well]. Joan is an excellent English teacher, and she's also working on her Master's as we speak."[155]

Other favorite instructors include Mrs. Tolese Green, who taught home economics; Mr. Clint Harley, who was a homeroom teacher, a science teacher, and a basketball coach; Mr. Varnell Norman, a music instructor; and Mr. Wesley Lambert, a science teacher. Wilson alum Jimmy Hunter praises Mr. Wilson and Mr. Norman for their generosity and expertise. Says Hunter, "Those people had the knowledge, and they were willing to give it to all of us." Like Samuel Bryant, Jimmy Hunter praises his instructors at A.A. Wilson for their commitment to providing students with classroom experiences and study skills that prepared them for college work. For Hunter, Mr. Lambert's instruction went far beyond the memorization of facts and frameworks. Instead, Lambert emphasized the importance of understanding the tools necessary for lifelong learning and success. Explains Hunter,

[P]eople like Wesley Lambert ... used his college degree to come back and teach us in a manner that you would be able to use in college, other than just learning how to remember stuff. There's a big difference between photographic memory and actually knowing what you are talking about. And he used that kind of system to teach us so that you could take almost anything and work with it ... In college you have blue book exams, that type of thing, and you don't have multiple choices and fill in the blank and that kind of thing. You might have one sentence, and that's your exam, but you had to expand on that sentence. Well I got that learning from people like Wesley Lambert here in Malvern.[156]

Also remembered fondly is Mrs. Dorothy Willis. She was Judy Pierce's seventh grade home economics teacher. "She was just so sweet," recalls Pierce, "but she was stern too," and "we learned so much from her."[157]

One of the most highly respected figures on the A.A. Wilson campus was Mr. Lindsey Henry, husband of Joan Henry, the beloved English teacher. The head coach of the Dragons football team, he is remembered as the man who established that football legacy. Rev. Henry Mitchell remembers Coach Henry as the man who "built some real pride in the athletic program."[158] Samuel Bryant remembers Coach Henry as a leader and an innovator whose playing strategies made him a standout throughout the region:

> Coach Henry was, at the time … one of the most offensive-minded coaches in this region. You couldn't beat him. He would always come up with a play. He was using counterplays, traps, tackle eligibles—he even had a formation that we called the cockeyed spread. And it was just incredible. The officials had to think, *was this legal*, because the opposing coach was like "Oh, I've never seen this before."[159]

Coach Henry's influence was not, however, limited to the playing field. For Bryant and other Dragons players he was not only an athletic coach, but a strong role model who provided guidance both on and off the field. John Hill explains: "[Coach Henry] instilled a lot of things in me—values, good, values … because he was there for us, and when we thought we couldn't do it, he said we could do it." For Hill, this leadership and encouragement "contributed a lot to [his] manhood," at a critical point in his life. Says the former Dragon, "[W]ithout him, one thing I know [is] we wouldn't have gone as far as we did."[160]

Like John Hill, Samuel Bryant remembers Coach Henry as valued mentor; and for many Dragons players, his mentorship off the field was even more critical to their development than his role as athletic coach. Bryant explains Henry's dual role:

> He was like a father figure for a lot of guys, because it was so many that came from one-parent homes. He was all about discipline. He made men out of boys, because when you got on that football team you were a boy, but when you left there you were a man, because it was just like going to the military.[161]

John Hill remembers Coach Henry as a strong-willed leader who was straightforward and persistent. Hill entered Wilson High School with the intention of joining the band, but Coach Henry saw that he had the ability to make a significant contribution to the football program and insisted that Hill come out for practice. Hill shares the story of how he went from a likely drummer in the Wilson band to Dragons football player:

[W]e had P.E. under [Coach Henry], and he told me, "I want you to come out this evening and get your uniform and I want to you play ball." And I didn't want to play football. I said, "it's not—that's not my thing." But coach was the type of guy [who], if he told you to do something, it's best you do it, because he would make P.E. a living hell for you ... I made up my mind—[said] "I'm not going, I'm going to band because I want to be a drummer ... I'm going to beat the skins." So I go in there, told Mr. Wilson [the music instructor] what I wanted to do and everything, and he said, "Okay, okay." [H]e gave me the band sticks and drum and I was sitting back there and ... all of a sudden Coach comes to the door and he says, "Mr. Wilson, is John Hill in there?" Mr. Wilson said, "Yeah, he's back there." And he didn't have to say too much of anything. [Coach Henry] just looked at me and I said, "Oh God, I dun messed up." So he got me out of there and he said, "I thought I told you to come out" ... [H]e said, "Get out there on the field." And that was the end of ... my drumming. I never became a drummer, but I played football for three years under him and don't regret it ... When coach spoke, you did what coach said. That's all that was. There was no talking back, [or] asking why; you just do it. That was it the way it was and I don't regret it, though I thank God for having been in his presence—I really do.[162]

A leader both on the field and off, Coach Henry transformed the lives of many of his players, providing a structure that instilled in them the value of hard work and the joys of competition. Not all of those who called him Coach, however, knew him for his work on the football field. Jimmy Hunter, who holds all of the basketball scoring records at A.A. Wilson High School, remembers Linsey Henry as a dynamic and inspiring coach for those who played their sport above the rim. He was as firm and demanding a leader for the Dragons basketball team as he was for the school football squad. "He was an individual [who] took no excuses, and he didn't want to hear anything about I *can't*," recalls Hunter, "because, in his words,

'You *can*—all you have to do is do it.'" For the high school basketball standout, those words were deeply influential. Says Hunter, "I took a lot of that lesson in life … and it made a big difference in my life."[163]

The teachers and coaches are not the only adults at A.A. Wilson who made a significant impact on students' lives. Cafeteria head Mrs. Merriweathers was as widely adored as any teacher or coach. "My mother, Alice Flanagan Merriweathers, was over the Hot Lunch Program at Malvern [Colored] High School," recalls Geraldine Sullivan (Malvern Colored High School, Class of 1946).[164] And, notes Dr. Samuel Benson, the hot lunch program in Malvern's black schools was started, "not by the government … but by the local women's clubs."[165] When the high school program moved to A.A. Wilson, Mrs. Merriweathers brought her prodigious culinary skills to the new building where, says Rev. Henry Mitchell, she "cooked the most delicious meals anyone could ever, ever dream of eating."[166]

While many Wilson alumni can recall with ease those teachers, administrators and staff who made their school years so memorable, few share the perspective of Laura Hunter (A.A. Wilson High School, Class of 1964). Hunter graduated from Wilson High School and then later returned to her alma mater as a novice teacher. She completed three years at Philander Smith College in Little Rock, Arkansas before returning to teach at Wilson for one year, "on a certificate." She then returned to Philander Smith to complete her final year of college. For Laura Hunter, teaching at A.A. Wilson was a singular pleasure. "It was wonderful [and] I loved it," she gushes. For Hunter, "it was just thoroughly enjoyable … working with the children." She took great pleasure in the opportunity to test and expand her teaching skills. "I was doing things that I didn't know I could do," she recalls. "I had not had all of my training for teaching; I had not done student teaching, so I was doing what I thought, teaching the way I thought I should teach, and it worked out." Having experienced A.A. Wilson as both student and teacher, Laura Hunter can say that she enjoyed both experiences equally. As a student, she built strong friendships and learned from skilled and passionate instructors. As a teacher, she shared her newly acquired knowledge, but she also continued to learn and grow, drawing on the passion and engagement of her students as well as from the experience and insights of her older colleagues. "It was really wonderful," Hunter recalls, "and I fully planned to be a teacher. I even had an offer to teach when it was time for me to graduate." The rapidly changing conditions of the period, however, would dictate otherwise. Explains Laura Hunter, "[A]ffirmative action came, and the doors opened, and I walked through the doors to ... other occupations."[167]

Photos

Taylor Henson, photographed in 1917.
(*The Crisis Magazine*, May 1917.)

"1865: Being Set Free"
By Lendora Williams Miles

We are African American.
Our ancestors came from Africa's land.
They knew naught about America.
They came here at their captor's command.

They came here tied and fettered.
And were believed to be of a savage race.
They could not escape from captivity
And they were sold for slaves.

For years our ancestors labored here.
They labored hard without their pay,
And were often sold, beaten, and mistreated,
Until freedom came that day.

When freedom came
Chains were broken that held them down,
And they walked away from vast plantations
Knowing they were freedom bound.

African Americans have made progress,
Since the day God set us free,
And we'll forever be grateful to God,
For granting us our liberty.

Dr. Samuel Benson, circa 1972.
(Collection of Dr. Samuel Benson.)

Eutah and Viola Jones photographed in their general store, circa
1930-1940s (top) and 1970s (bottom). (Collection of Billy Earl Jones.)

Principal Edward E. Bailey.
(Collection of Dorothy Baker.)

Photo of early Malvern area residents. Dorothulia,
Roy, and Ezra were ancestors of Malvern Colored
High School alumna Dorothy Baker.
(Collection of Dorothy Baker.)

Early photo of Malvern and Perla Teachers.
(Collection of Dorothy Baker.)

Ancestors of Dorothy Baker standing on the
porch of their Malvern area home.
(Collection of Dorothy Baker.)

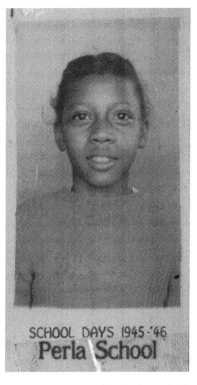 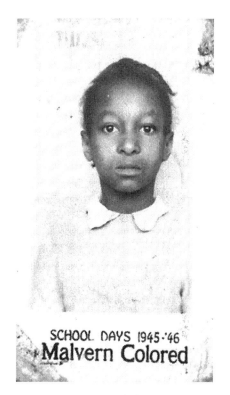

Dorothy Baker (left) and Anna Jean Owens (right).
(Left to right, collection of Dorothy Baker and
collection of Joe Paul Owens.)

Malvern resident Claude Ella Willis.
(Collection of Jewell Willis, Jr.)

Malvern area teachers and spouses Clifford Walsh (high school) and Lois Walsh (elementary school), photographed in 1955. (Collection of Exie Carroll.)

Malvern Colored High School alumni and area business
owners and Charlie and Exie Carroll.
(Collection of Exie Carroll.)

Malvern Colored High School graduate and Richmond,
CA city councilman Richard L. Griffin.
(Collection of Bettye Griffin.)

Photo of early Malvern residents. Dennis and Nellie
Nolan appear on the far left.
(Collection of Louise Williams.)

Malvern Colored High School boys basketball team
with Coach L. Johnson (back row).
(Collection of the Curtis Wiggins family.)

Rating Scale

Name Of School _Malvern Elem._ Grade _1_
Name Of Student _Owens, Joe Paul_ Teacher _Mrs. L. Walsh_

Scholastic Ability (or progress)	very seldom	part of time	nearly always
I. Reading - Literature			
1. Shows interest in reading.			✓
2. Reads with understanding.			✓
3. Reads well orally.			✓
4. Reads without pointing.			✓
5. Learns new words.			✓
II. Language - Spelling			
1. Tells own experiences clearly.			✓
2. Uses correct written form.			✓
3. Spells correctly words used.			✓
III. Numbers - Writing - Health			
1. Learns number skills of his grade.			✓
2. Depends on himself in written work.			✓
3. Reasons well in solving problems.			✓
4. Writes neatly.			✓
Traits, Habits, and Attitudes			
I. Work Habits			
1. I listen and follow directions carefully and promptly.			✓
2. I work independently and carefully.			✓
3. I share work and play materials with others.			✓

Perla Sherriff Joe Paul Owens' report card from his first
grade year at Malvern Colored Elementary School.
His instructor was Mrs. Lois Walsh.
(Collection of Joe Pal Owens.)

A.A. Wilson High School teacher Mrs. Joan Henry.
(Wilson Dragons yearbook.)

Malvern Colored and A.A. Wilson High
School teacher Mrs. Henrietta Bailey.
(Wilson Dragons yearbook.)

A school-aged Joe Paul Owens, photographed in Malvern.
(Collection of Joe Paul Owens.)

Malvern Colored High School photo of Jewell "Pete" Willis, Jr.
(Collection of Jewell Willis Jr.)

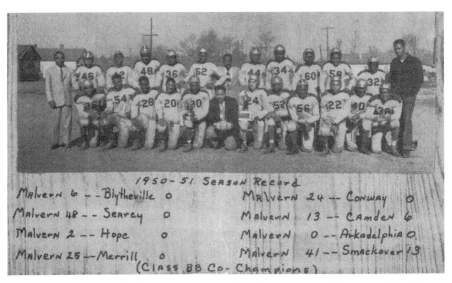

1950-51 Season Record

Malvern 6 -- Blytheville 0   Malvern 24 -- Conway 0
Malvern 48 -- Searcy 0   Malvern 13 -- Camden 6
Malvern 2 -- Hope 0   Malvern 0 -- Arkadelphia 0
Malvern 25 -- Merrill 0   Malvern 41 -- Smackover 13
(Class BB Co-Champions)

Malvern Colored High School football team, photographed
with Coach Johnson and Principal Horace Jones.
(Collection of Jewell Willis, Jr.)

Principal and teacher Sophronia Tuggle, for whom
Tuggle Elementary School was named.
(Collection of Jewell Willis, Jr.)

Malvern Colored High School Band, photographed in 1951.
(Collection of Jewell Willis, Jr.)

Wilson High School. (Wilson Dragons yearbook.)

Wilson High School Cheerleaders, 1964.
(Wilson Dragons Yearbook.)

1964 Wilson High School Girls Senior Basketball
Team with Coach Mrs. Dorothy Willis.
(Wilson Dragons Yearbook.)

1954 Wilson High School Dragons Football Team.
(Wilson Dragons Yearbook.)

A.A. Wilson High School. (Wilson Dragons Yearbook.)

Acme Brick Company, 1940. (Library of Congress.)

Hot Springs Railroad Station, photographed
in the late 19th century.
(Library of Congress.)

Chapter IV

Integration and Beyond:

The Malvern-Wilson Reunions and the End of "Colored" Schools

"I came home one evening. It was probably in the beginning of the fall before school, probably around August or June, and my parents say, 'Sit down son we got something that we want you to do.'"

—Alvin Murdoch, Malvern Senior
High School, Class of 1968

The members of the Class of 1968 were the last students in Malvern and Perla to receive diplomas from A.A. Wilson; and their commencement, in June of that year, marked not only the closing of Malvern's African American high school, but the end of a rich and cherished tradition of black secondary education, one that had been a source of pride throughout the community. In its integration plan, the Malvern School Board called for the closure of the city's black high school and the transfer of all of its students to the previously all-white Malvern Senior High School so that, beginning in August of 1968, all of the city's high school-aged students, of all races and ethnicities, would learn, play, study, and eat together in the same building, for the first time in Malvern history.

For those African American students who entered Malvern High School in the fall of 1968, any positive feelings—about being at the vanguard of a new dispensation, about making Malvern and Arkansas history, or about the possibility of new friends and new opportunities—were tempered by the grief of losing an institution that, for the previous 23 years, had functioned as the center of black community life. For many former Wilson students, the move to Malvern Senior High School meant the demise of the place that had shaped so many of their dreams and aspirations. As elementary students they had fantasized about one day becoming a Dragon—on the football field, on the basketball court, in the marching band, with the majorettes, on the cheerleading squad, or by applying the fearless Dragon spirit to their academic work. And as fully-fledged Wilson High students, they dreamed of graduating from a school that belonged to them and to their community. Black students who entered Malvern Senior High School in the fall of 1968 began their school year without the support of the institution that had nurtured them. Their only choice was to steel their nerves, master their resentments, push through their grief, draw deeply on their Dragon pride, and move forward.

This was the reality of integration for all of those students who were enrolled at Wilson during the 1967-68 school year, except, of course, the graduating seniors. There was, however, another group—a previous group—whose transfer from their beloved Wilson into the unknown that was Malvern Senior High was not dictated by the will of the school board but was, instead, a decision made by their parents. For these students, their apprehension and grief was mingled with an irony that, at times, felt absurdly cruel. Alvin Murdoch was one of a pilot group of seven young men and women who, in the fall of 1966, became the first black students to enter Malvern Senior High. For the next two years, these seven students lived with the painful knowledge that the teachers and coaches, the staff and— most importantly—the friends who they loved were still at Wilson, enjoying the daily rhythm of academic life at the high school that the African American community had created for its children. Their departure from Wilson was a choice that isolated them from the majority of their peers. They were the seven for whom the Wilson marching band would never play and to whom Mrs. Merriweathers and her successors would never serve another home-style meal. While the full integration of Malvern's public school system, in 1968, was a shared experience that united all of those for whom Wilson had felt like home, the pilot integration created pariahs of the four girls and three boys who entered Malvern Senior High School in the fall of 1966, if not in the minds of their peers, then certainly in their own minds and, more importantly, in their hearts.

In Alvin Murdoch's home, the decision that he would leave Wilson for Malvern High was made by his parents. He still remembers the otherwise uneventful summer evening when his parents called him over, saying, "Sit down, son, we got something that we want you to do." Murdoch recalls sitting down with his parents to complete the application to change schools; but then, as now, he knew little of the political machinations that brought about what felt like an abrupt change in what had always been a segregated system. Looking back on that summer night, Murdoch imagines that, "every kid … that went to the all black school got an application," and that the application represented "a freedom of choice" offered up by the board, "in order to change [the] schools." In his household, however, the choice was Murdoch's parents', not his. "We filled [the application] out," recalls Murdoch, "and it wasn't 'would you' or 'could you'; [it was] 'you're going.'"[168]

The young Alvin Murdoch almost immediately grasped the scope of this impending change in his education. "I had to come to [the] realization," he explains, "that, while I was going into a different world, I [was] going to lose my friends; I [was] going to lose the direction we were going." At the time, he took some comfort in the fact that the same friends with whom he would no longer be attending school "were your Sunday school friends, were your church friends, [and] they were your neighborhood friends." He was, however, keenly aware that, on Monday mornings at school, he would see "a bunch of different kids that [he] had no ties to for [his] first ten years of education."[169]

The memory of that first year at Malvern High School remains fresh in Alvin Murdoch's mind, and he describes the experience of being one of its first seven black students in sharp detail:

> The first day I can see vividly … We [the seven Wilson students] planned to get there at the same time. I actually picked up a few, because I had transportation; and we entered the school without any idea of what we were going to see, what we were going to feel or hear. [The] school body had assembled, and there were some jeers, but there wasn't

any outright violence or nothing like that ... I think the white students might have been more curious [than anything else]. I don't think it was a mob; it was just an overflow. It was a large crowd which seemed to us as overpowering because there were just seven of us. And it seemed like the whole student body [was there]. You don't have a picture of the whole school. You walk up a set of steps and you walk into the main building and there were classes to the right and that whole hall—that whole area—was full of kids. And to us it seemed threatening, but [there was] no violence or nothing. Like I said, there was a few unpleasant words towards us ... but there wasn't anything physical, nothing thrown, no attack or nothing like that ... there was a few that did some things that were inappropriate but they were kids too.[170]

During the coming school year, there were many challenges, as the former Wilson students—who came to be called the Malvern Seven—struggled with both the racism of some of their white peers and the pain of being separated from the friends and teachers they had known. Still, there were some positive moments during that initial year. Alvin Murdoch describes a surprising instance of solidarity between him and his white teammates:

Being football players and traveling through different towns [to] play football, I experienced different forms of taunting and name calling ... In one instance ... we were playing Camden and the restaurant owner didn't want to serve me, and I have to say this because I try to be truthful in how I talk. The football boys decided they weren't going to eat either, so then I guess that's when we pretty well came together as a team. So, the manager of the restaurant, I guess he was looking at the revenue he lost. He had to make amends, and I thought that was a good gesture from the coaches and the kids on the football team. They stood up for what they thought was right.[171]

For at least that one night, the manager of the restaurant relented and chose to serve all of the football players, including Murdoch. "I don't know if it solved a lot of problems in the Camden area," opines Murdoch, "but, for that night, he had to change his philosophy on race."[172]

Despite improved relations with his teammates, as evidenced in the incident described above, Murdoch never developed a full sense of belonging at his new school. While commencement at A.A. Wilson brought the entire community together—friends, clergy, extended family, neighbors—to celebrate its graduating seniors, Malvern Senior High School restricted the number of guests each student could bring to its commencement ceremonies. "[Y]ou couldn't have all your uncles and aunties and your cousins and all there," recalls Murdoch, "you just had your immediate family." For Alvin Murdoch and the other graduating black students, this represented a dramatic departure from the graduation ceremony at Wilson; and the isolation of the students was only compounded by the fact that they were graduating from a different school and with different classmates than those with whom they had begun their high school journey. Murdoch and his small handful of black classmates "missed that euphoria and the [sense that] we finished—we started this race [and] we finished together." Says Murdoch, "Not having someone to lean on ... we marched and we moved on."[173]

Late in the spring of 1968, nearly two years after Alvin Murdoch first learned that he would not be returning to A.A. Wilson High, the announcement was made to all enrolled Wilson students that their school would be dissolved and that all but the graduating seniors would be transferred to Malvern Senior High. Many of the students and their families were informed of this impending change through the local press. "They didn't tell us, [and] they didn't tell our parents," recalls Judy Pierce. Instead, "They put it in the newspaper, and that's where we read it, that [in] September we were going to school at Malvern Senior High."[174] The consensus among those A.A. Wilson alumni who were enrolled at the time of desegregation is that none of them wanted to leave their school behind. "[I]t was a hurting experience to know that [Wilson] was going to be shut down," recalls Rev. Henry Mitchell. "We knew [we were not] going to be able to graduate here, and that took a lot out of us."[175]

Both students and their community were deeply invested in the activities, events, traditions, and rituals that had come to shape and give substance to the "colored" high school experience in Malvern and Perla. For then Wilson student Judy Pierce, the closing of Wilson High put an end to her hopes for senior honors in the activities that had been such an important part of her life. Explains Pierce, "I really just had a wonderful time in my high school years, except one year, and that's when they integrated us." A member of the A.A. Wilson choir, Pierce was "up for recital in the eleventh grade," and she was also "going to get honors for being a cheerleader and [for] being in the band. Then, that summer, they took us away."[176]

For John Hill, the disbanding of Wilson High meant the end of Dragon football, a painful loss not only for him and his teammates, but also for Coach Henry, from whom Hill learned of the impending school closure. He can still describe in stark detail the moment that he and his teammates learned of the plan to dissolve A.A. Wilson and transfer its students:

> [C]oach, he was sitting in his office and he wasn't saying very much. You know, it wasn't like him, but we didn't know what was going on. And he called us all in and told us, "I need to talk to you guys" ... [N]ormally, when he calls us, we've done something. And so I said, "Oh boy! We in trouble. Somebody done did something." And, you know, he's the type [who], if one do wrong and he don't know who did it, everybody paid for it. So, he sat down and he began to kind of sniffle, and I knew something was wrong then, because he wasn't that type ... I never seen him shed a tear; and he said, "this will be our last year here." And I said, "What?" You know, everybody just sat there with their mouths open ... because we had planned on having a great year, the [next year], because you know that year we had lost one senior and we had lost I think two games that year and that was it, so we were coming back. We were going to come back and be tough; but he told us, he said, "This will be the last year that we will be at Wilson. We'll be together at Senior High." And he said, "I know it's hard for all of us, but we got to do what we got to do. We got to make the transition." And, for the first time, he said (because he always taught us, [that] men don't cry) ... he said "Everybody sit down. If you want to cry, let it out." But we all—all of us did, and we just ... had no idea what we were facing—what we were going to have to face when we got [to Malvern Senior High].[177]

For Judy Pierce, attending Malvern Senior High felt like being put "in a jail cell ... because," she explains, "just think of a place that you've never been before and all the people are doing one thing and you're totally different; and you get into this place where you don't feel that you're welcome ... and you're thrown in there without saying 'I want to go.'"[178] For some former Wilson students, the feeling that they were not welcome was affirmed by the behaviors and words of their white classmates. John Hill remembers the first year at Malvern Senior High School as "a living hell," due in no small part to what he experienced as persistent harassment from white students, some of whom were as resentful about the amalgamation of Malvern's secondary programs as their African American counterparts were grief-stricken.[179]

Much of this resentment played itself out in humiliating words and pranks. "They spit on us, and stuff like that," recalls John Hill. "We'd go down on the first floor for classes," he recalls, "and they would get up on the second floor and spit down on top of our heads." This routine was both enraging and humiliating for the former Wilson students, but the school administration provided little assistance in addressing the practice. Says Hill, "When you'd go to the class principal, they'd play it off like 'well, we don't know who did it.'" Feeling unprotected by their school administrators, some former Wilson students chose to address the persistent taunts and harassment with their fists, a response that, Hill now realizes, provided a convenient justification for expelling some of the school's recently enrolled young black men. Although he would go on to earn his diploma from Malvern Senior High, Hill notes that, "Many others didn't graduate ... because they pushed us and we played into their hands ... and got ... expelled for fighting and different things."[180] Even today, more than 40 years since the closure of Malvern Senior High, Hill believes that the inaction of the school administration during that turbulent time was part of a deliberate plan to thin the numbers of the enrolled black students. Says Hill, "As I look back on it now, it [the principal's inaction] was designed to get us kicked out. They wanted us to act a fool so that they could put us out."[181]

Hill's experience in his predominantly white physical education class exemplifies this tension-filled dynamic:

> [I]t was in P.E., and we had a tag team match ... These white guys had pads on their knees and they played their part wrestling. So it was our time to get on the mat. So when we got ready to get on the mat they thought, "no, we're not going to let you get up here," in so many words. So we decided—we had a nasty attitude ... that we were going to show you. We're going to wrestle. You all done had your turn, we gon' wrestle. So when we started, Coach Abby came out and he's asking questions about whom, why were we doing what we were doing, and I

told him, I said, "Man, it's our time to wrestle" ... And we teamed up and wrestled each other. And so he told me, he said, "This is my gym," in so many words, "and I say what goes." I said, "No we gon' wrestle." And so I guess he took it offensive [and] him and two other coaches were going to take me back there and they were going to beat me ... they were going to give me a beating to put me in my place.[182]

Coach Henry arrived at the gymnasium as these events were unfolding, and he intervened on behalf of the former Wilson football player, as Hill describes in the following recollection:

Coach Henry said, "What's going on?" I told him, [and] Coach Abby told him what had happened and ... Coach [Henry] said, "Well, I'll tell you what. Let me deal with him." He said, "I'll take care of him." He said, "You know better." He pointed it out there in front of them ... and when they all left ... we sat down. He said, "Man, ya'll need to cool it." He said, "You all are playing into their hands." He said, "They want you to act a fool, so they can get rid of you." And he gave me a talk for about 20 minutes. [Then] he said, "Now, I'm going to take this board and I'm going to hit this desk and I want you to get out of here and don't fall for their tricks no more." He said, "Now, when you walk out you act just like you've been beaten." And I did. I walked out. And that's just the kind of man he was. He was good. And from this day up until now they don't know what went on in that dressing room, but he never touched me. He showed me. He said it with tears in his eyes. He said, "They don't want you here, they don't want you here." And they didn't want him there, and at that time we played into their hands, a lot of us, many of us.[183]

When former A.A. Wilson students attempted to resume, at Malvern Senior High, the extracurricular activities in which they had participated at their previous school, the reception they received conveyed more subtly the same resentment towards their presence that spitting and other forms of harassment expressed overtly. Judy Pierce's experiences with the cheerleading squad exemplified the loss of status and community that so deeply colored her one year at the newly integrated school. The Malvern Senior High choir willingly made room for their new students but, recalls Pierce, the cheerleading squad was closed to new membership, and "even though we got a chance to be in the school choir, they already had their cheerleaders, [and] so we didn't get a chance to do that." "They did ask us what were some of our cheers," Pierce recalls, "and we would show them, and they liked it because, you know, we were always a little sassy; but we didn't get a chance to cheer ... we got a chance to show them our cheers."[184]

For Judy Pierce and for many of the other students who were transferred out of Wilson, the experience of entering Malvern Senior High School, "kind of took away all the things that we had so hoped for, ... all the honors that we had, [and] everything that we had worked so hard for in A.A. Wilson High [and] we ended up with nothing."[185] "When I was young," admits Pierce, "I used to be really angry about it; but after I grew up I could see that ... you have to start somewhere, so why not with us?" This understanding, however, came only later in life. Observes Pierce, "As a child or as a young adult, you look at those things that ... was taken away from you, and that's what we felt; we felt that things were taken away from us."[186]

Separated from the close-knit and supportive community that had encouraged and celebrated their achievements, and stripped of their leadership roles in so many of the teams and organizations that had shaped their years at A.A. Wilson, the black students who entered Malvern Senior High School in fall of 1968 experienced school integration more as the fatal blow to an institution they treasured than as a net gain in opportunity. And these feelings of deprivation and loss were based on something far more profound than homesickness or nostalgia. While integration is remembered as the moment at which African Americans were able to leave behind ineffective and underfunded public schools for the wealthier, more generously resourced schools that had previously excluded them, the black students of Malvern felt no such inadequacy. On the contrary, both A.A. Wilson students and their parents cherished and respected the teachers, coaches, and staff of their school as well as the education they provided. While many— even most—black secondary schools in the segregated south were woefully underfunded and sent few if any students on to 2- and 4-year colleges and universities, the college preparatory curriculum at A.A. Wilson and its predecessor, Malvern Colored High School, equipped a generation of black Malvern and Perla residents for a lifetime of success in the full range of academic, professional, and individual pursuits.

The Birth of the Malvern-Wilson Reunions

In the 23 years that Malvern offered a full high school program to its African American students (at Malvern Colored High School, from 1945-1952, and at A.A. Wilson High School, from 1952-1968), the community produced black graduates who would go on to become doctors, attorneys, primary and secondary school teachers, college professors, actors and actresses, members of the clergy, writers, politicians, judges, business owners, and community activists, not only in Malvern and surrounding areas, but across the United States.

Malvern's black high schools produced far too many distinguished alumni to name them all in this slim volume. In addition, when we take into account the numbers of Malvern Colored and A.A. Wilson graduates who did the hard and essential work of transmitting the values and lessons of their teachers and mentors to their children and grandchildren, then virtually all of those who attended those schools must certainly be counted among those alumni of whom the community is rightfully proud. Indeed, a brief examination of the achievements of the scion of Malvern and Wilson graduates is as clear an indication as any that the spirit and values of Malvern Colored and A.A. Wilson high schools live on.

The distinguished men and women profiled in the following list serve, then, as only a small sample of much larger community of Malvern and Wilson alumni who have used their talents and abilities to improve the fortunes of their families, their communities, and the nation:

Dorothy Baker: Dorothy Baker was born in Little Rock, Arkansas in 1936. The fifteenth and only surviving child of her father, a painter for the Southern Pacific Railroad Company, Baker was only six months old when he died. Eventually, Baker's mother, a native of Perla, returned to her hometown with her daughter, just in time to enroll young Dorothy in Malvern's "colored" school system. After graduating from Malvern Colored High School, she enrolled at what is now the University of Arkansas, Pine Bluff. In the late 1950s, after completing her bachelor's degree, she relocated to the San Francisco Bay Area to join her husband who had moved to California seeking work. Baker's career as a lifelong educator began shortly after her children entered preschool. After earning a second degree in early childhood development, she began working in Berkeley and Oakland preschool and child development programs. She would go on to earn a master's degree in education with an emphasis on learning development from Holy Names College, after which she served as a learning skills and reading development specialist at a number of programs, including Edward Shand's Adult School, Burckhalter Elementary School, Allendale Elementary School, and Roosevelt Junior High School. Dorothy Baker retired from teaching at the age of 55. After the death of her husband, Dorothy Baker embarked on a second career. She completed seminary studies at the Claremont School of Theology and the Pacific School of Religion. A member of Downs Memorial United Methodist Church, Rev. Baker was consecrated as a diaconal minister of the church in 1999, she was ordained as a Deacon there in 2001, after which she was appointed an Associate Pastor. She served in that post until 2007 when she retired from the ministry.

Fran Bennett: Born in Malvern in 1937, Bennett is leading a successful career as both an actress of stage and screen and a sought-after acting instructor. She holds a B.S. and an M.A. from the University of Wisconsin, Madison. She served as the voice and movement director for the Guthrie Theater in Minneapolis for 12 years. In addition, she has led voice production workshops at the University of Mississippi, the University of Wisconsin, the University of Minnesota, Iowa State University, Fisk University, Carnegie Mellon University, and the London Academy of Music and Dramatic Arts. From 1996 to 2003, Bennett served as the Head of Acting and Director of Performance at CalArts School of Theater, and she is currently a Master Voice Teacher with the Massachusetts-based Shakespeare & Company. Though she is highly-regarded as a skilled teacher of voice and movement, audiences are most familiar with her work as a television and movie actress. Bennett has played guest roles on *In the Heat of the Night*, *Quantum Leap, and Star Trek: The Next Generation*, the films *Wes Craven's Newest Nightmare*, *8MM*, and many others. She currently has a recurring role on NBC's *The Book of Daniel*. In 2005, the mayor of Malvern declared August 7 of that year Fran Bennett Day.

Dr. Samuel Benson: The son of Malvern area business owner Frances Calhoun, the grandson of pioneering entrepreneur Tillie Yancy Benson Graham (on his father's side), and the great-grandson of landholder Taylor Henson (on his mother's side), Dr. Benson has continued his family's legacy of using business and property ownership to achieve economic stability and provide opportunities for the larger community. A gifted student in mathematics and the sciences, Dr. Benson graduated from Malvern Colored High School in 1952. He went on to earn both an M.D. and a Ph.D. (in Physiology and Pharmacology) from the University of Nebraska. He completed his internship in Psychiatry and Internal Medicine at New York's Bellevue Hospital and his residency in Psychiatry at the Stanford University Hospital. He served on the clinical faculty at Stanford's medical school and as a lecturer at Stanford's law school for 11 years, from 1975 to 1986. Dr. Benson has served as an expert witness in a number of landmark court cases throughout the state of California, as the medical director for the Central Methadone Clinic in San Jose, and as President of Medical Staff for CPC Walnut Creek Hospital. His work in community health earned him an appointment to the Advisory Health Council for the California Department of Health. Dr. Benson is the founder and president of the Registry of Physician Specialists, as well as the founder and CEO of the Registry Foundation and the Henson Benson Foundation. The Registry Foundation provides educational funding and support to former inmates, and the Henson Benson Foundation supports research and media initiatives to preserve and raise awareness of the rich historical and cultural legacy of Malvern, Arkansas. The foundation also supports educational programs and scholarship for Malvern area youth.

Exie Carroll: A graduate of Malvern Colored High School and the owner of Exie's, a clothing boutique in Malvern, Carroll is one of Malvern's long-term African American business owners. Her store maintains an inventory of high-quality women's clothing and accessories. Hers is one of the first black-owned stores to occupy retail space on the city's Main Street. She has held positions of responsibility in a number of community organizations, including the Malvern Chamber of Commerce, the Hot Spring County Medical Center Board of Directors, and others.

Charles "Charlie" Carroll: A 1952 graduate of Malvern Colored High School, Carroll attended junior college in Little Rock for only a short time before he was drafted into the armed services. After completing a 2-year tour of duty, he returned to Arkansas and enrolled at Little Rock Barber College. After receiving his license, he was apprenticed to Mr. Lacey Harvey, a longtime barbershop owner who was also his former history teacher. After three years of working for Harvey, Carroll established his own shop. He has since been the proprietor of Carroll Barbershop, a trusted fixture in the city's business landscape. A long-term Malvern resident, Carroll has demonstrated his commitment to the community not only through his role as a business owner, but also through his work as a member of both the City Board of Governors and the Henson Benson Foundation Board of Directors. He has been married to Exie Carroll, his high school sweetheart, since 1954.

Dr. Ted Carroll: The salutatorian of the A.A. Wilson High School Class of 1959, Dr. Carroll attended Coalinga Junior College (now West Hills College, Coalinga) in Northern California. There he won awards for both his academic achievements and his athletic accomplishments. All-American Junior College football player, he went on to earn bachelor's and master's degrees in both physical education and English literature, and six secondary education and administration credentials, all from San Francisco State University. After earning a doctorate in education from the University of California, Berkeley, Dr. Carroll began what would become a distinguished career as a teacher and administrator in the San Francisco Public School system. In 1971, at the age of 29, he became the youngest principal in San Francisco Public School History, when he was hired to lead and revive Pelton Junior High, a middle school in the city's troubled Bayview-Hunters Point neighborhood. He would occupy that post for 12 years. His success in changing student outcomes and attitudes at the school was covered by many local and national media outlets, including <u>Ebony Magazine</u>, <u>New Yorker Magazine</u>, the <u>San Francisco Chronicle</u>, and many others. Dr. Carroll's commitment to San Francisco Bay Area minority youth is evident in his extensive record of community involvement and activism. He has served on the Bayview-Hunters Point Coordinating Council and the Mission Latinos Organization Board of Directors, and he has held leadership positions in Young Community Developers, Inc. and other San Francisco non-profit organizations geared toward youth training and development. In addition to his work in education and community organizing, he has also established himself in the field of real estate, as a mortgage broker, remodeler, and property manager.

Raner Collins: After graduating from Wilson High School, Hon. Raner Christercunean Collins earned a B.A. from Arkansas Polytechnic Institute and a J.D. from the University of Arizona College of Law. After working first as a clerk and then as a trial attorney for the Pima County Attorney's Office, he served briefly as the magistrate for the City of Tucson Court before accepting a post as one of Pima's county attorneys. He served as a Pima County Superior Court judge pro tempore from 1985 to 1988 and as Pima County Superior Court Judge from 1988 to 1998. That year he accepted an appointment from Bill Clinton to fill a vacant seat on the United States District Court from the District of Arizona. He has served in that position since his confirmation on August 3, 1998.

Dr. Patricia L. Greene Griffen: A graduate of Wilson High School, Dr. Griffen established Clinical Psychology Services, Inc., in 1983. She maintained this independent practice for more than 25 years. After completing her bachelor's degree in psychology at Ouachita Baptist College, from which she graduated *magna cum laude*, she went on to earn an M.A. in clinical psychology from the University of Arkansas, Fayetteville. She worked as a psychologist at Pike's Peak Family Counseling and Mental Health Center in Colorado Springs, Colorado and as an instructor in the Department of Psychology at El Paso Community College in Texas before returning to her home state to enroll in the doctoral program in clinical psychology at the University of Arkansas. There she became the first African American to earn a Ph.D in that field. After graduating, she served, for a time, as a faculty member in the same department, before leaving to establish her own private practice. Dr. Griffen has held a number of leadership positions in her field, including: Director of Psychological Services for Adolescent Inpatient Treatment for the Arkansas Mental Health Services Division;

Director of South Pulaski Services for Central Arkansas Mental Health Services; and Psychological Consultant for the Restore Drug, Chemical Dependency, and Eating Disorder program at Riverview Hospital and St. Vincent Medical Infirmary in Little Rock. Dr. Griffen was appointed by then governor Bill Clinton to the Arkansas Board of Examiners in Psychology, where she served as chair, and she also served as the chair of the Arkansas Commitment Parents Advisory Board. She is currently a staff psychologist for the St. Vincent Medical Infirmary and the Baptist Health Medical Center, both in Little Rock.

Richard Griffin: Richard Lee Griffin was born in 1934, in Malvern, Arkansas. He served in the United States Army during which time he was stationed in Europe. Upon returning to the U.S., he enrolled in Philander Smith College where he met his wife, Bettye. After completing his baccalaureate studies, Griffin and his wife relocated to Richmond, California. He went on to earn his master's degree in education from San Francisco State University. After working as a microbiologist for Schlitz Brewery and as chief chemist for General Dynamics Corporation, he served for more than 20 years as a junior high school teacher and principal in the Oakland Unified School District. He went on to serve on the Richmond City Council for a 21-year period spanning from 1985 to 2006. As a city council member, Griffin was known for his commitment to improving living conditions for all Richmond residents as well as for his warm personality and infectious smile. A community activist as well as politician, he served as director of both the Richmond Girls Club and the Greater Richmond Social Service Corporation.

Bishop Carruth Hall: Born in Malvern in 1930, Bishop Carruth Hall has served as pastor of the Greater St. Paul Church of God in Christ (COGIC) in Las Vegas for more than 40 years. In October of 1993, he was appointed as Prelate of the First Ecclesiastical Jurisdiction of Nevada for the Church of God in Christ denomination, and he has held that post ever since. Prior to his current appointment, he served as the Las Vegas District Superintendent for the church. From 1994-2001, Bishop Hall was the General Assembly Sergeant at Arms for COGIC's

Nevada State Jurisdiction. Ordained in 1957, he is the founder of the Spiritual Renewal Ministries and St. Paul Bible College. He is a past president of C.H. Mason Bible College. In Hot Spring County, in 1949, at the age of 19, he married Loyce Aretha Wright, his wife of more than 60 years. The two have five children.

Gerald Jordan: A graduate of Wilson High School, Jordan is an Associate Professor in the Walter J. Lemke Department of Journalism at the University of Arkansas, his alma mater. In 1971, Jordan earned a master's in journalism from Northwestern University. In 1982 he was a Nieman Fellow at Harvard University. In 1995 he joined the faculty of the University of Arkansas. He has written for a number of news outlets including The Kansas City Star, The Boston Globe, and The Philadelphia Inquirer, where he served as a Washington correspondent, an assigning editor, and the North Zone editor.

Yvonne D. English Lovelace: Born in Waterbury, Connecticut in 1947, Yvonne Lovelace enrolled in Malvern's African American public school system after her family relocated to Arkansas. She attended Wilson High School where she was a varsity cheerleader and a member of the women's basketball and track teams. An athletic standout, Lovelace won a sports scholarship to Arkansas Agricultural, Mechanical, and Normal University (now the University of Arkansas at Pine Bluff). There she was a double major, earning Bachelor of Science degrees in both mathematics and chemistry. The salutatorian of her graduating class, she was voted "most talented" by her peers. A student-athlete in both college and high school, Lovelace was a prominent member of her college basketball, volleyball, and track teams (for which she earned the women's college record for the 100-yard dash). After graduation, Lovelace was recruited to teach at Tech Junior High in Omaha, Nebraska. She would go on to teach at Horace Mann High School before transferring to Benson High School in January of 1976. An instructor in the math department as well as the girls' volleyball coach, she was named Benson High School Teacher of the Year for the 1976-1977 school year. Yvonne D. English Lovelace died on January 10, 1991.

Rev. Henry Mitchell: The founder and pastor of Victory Praise and Worship Church in Malvern, a non-profit community organization affiliated with the Mount Willow Baptist Church, Rev. Mitchell attended A.A. Wilson High School before transferring to, and graduating from, Malvern Senior High School. After graduation he worked for Sears, during which time he also served as a youth minister. After he retired from Sears, with 17 years of experience as member of the clergy, Rev. Mitchell started the Victory Praise and Worship Church. A strong presence in the Malvern and Perla region, the church touches many lives throughout the community with its outreach initiatives and events. One of Rev. Mitchell's most important programs is the annual Back-to-School Youth Explosion. Open to children and teens, the event provides free school supplies, a free haircut, and continental breakfast for each child, followed by motivational speakers (like former Arkansas Razorback and San Francisco 49ers linebacker Vincent Bradford, a 1990 graduate of Malvern Senior High). Rev. Mitchell has been widely recognized for his work. Among his most recent honors is the Kristi Parker Norris Leadership Award, presented to him by the Malvern Chamber of Commerce, in recognition of his outstanding service to the youth of the community.

Joe Paul Owens: Perla Chief of Police Owens attended Wilson High School and graduated from Malvern Senior High School. He began his law enforcement career as an officer in the Malvern police department. In 1989, Sergeant Owens was one of three African American officers who filed a federal lawsuit alleging that they were overlooked for advancement because of their race and that less qualified white officers were granted promotions in their place. Of the three black officers who filed the complaint, Owens was the only one who remained in the department's employ. He would go on to complete more than two decades of distinguished service to the Malvern community before leaving to become the Perla Chief of Police. Despite the small size of his jurisdiction, Chief Owens has been involved in arrests and investigations that have attracted statewide media attention.

Thelma Pickens: A member of the A.A. Wilson High School Class of 1967, Thelma Pickens holds a degree from Brian's Business College (BBC) in Hot Springs, Arkansas. In 1968, while enrolled there, she became the first African American hired at the K-Mart store in that city. After completing her program at BBC, Pickens returned to Malvern, where she became the first African American hired at Gibson's Discount Center. At both stores, she held the highly visible position of cashier. Today Pickens is a Donor Services Representative at Heifer International, a prominent global non-profit dedicated to the elimination of hunger and poverty. She has been an employee at this Little Rock-based organization since 1999. Pickens was part of a 2005 delegation of Heifer International donor services staff members who were sent to Honduras to visit the organization's agricultural projects in that region. An avid collector of antiques, she has traveled to antique dealers and selling venues throughout the southern and eastern United States. Thelma Pickens is the mother of two daughters and she has two grandchildren, a boy and a girl.

Harry Roberson, Jr.: A graduate of Malvern Colored High School, Roberson used the academic and athletic skills he honed as a Malvern student-athlete to pay his way through Philander Smith College. He put his intellectual talents and strong work habits to use as a personal assistant to President M.L. Harris, in exchange for which the College paid his tuition. He used his athletic skills to play for the college's football team, in exchange for which he received room and board. After completing his undergraduate degree in business, Roberson relocated to Cleveland where he quickly found employment as a salesman with the Dunbar Life Insurance Company. His tenure there was interrupted after only six months, however, when he was drafted into United States Army. He would serve a 21-month tour of duty in Japan and Korea before returning to the U.S. In 1967, Roberson completed a master's degree in Urban Housing and Finance at the University of Pittsburg, and within five years he was employed in the Program Planning Office in Washington, D.C. After a short time, he was transferred to the U.S. Department of Labor where he worked until his retirement, in 1999. His only time away from the Department of Labor was during the two years that he served on the Arkansas Manpower Council (1975-1977).

In 1989, he received the Philander Smith Distinguished Alumni Award; and, in 1993, he was recognized with the U.S. Department of Labor Distinguished Career Service Award. In 1998, Roberson established a $26,000 endowed scholarship fund at Philander Smith. He has since been inducted into the College's prestigious M.L. Harris Society, in recognition of his generous record of giving.

Leo Ross: The youngest of four children, Leo Ross was born in Malvern, Arkansas. His father, Will Ross, worked in the brick and lumber industries and his mother was a domestic. His family also owned Will Ross and Sons, a small community grocery store. A talented musician, Ross was a saxophone player in the Wilson Dragons Marching Band. Gifted intellectually as well as musically, he was the valedictorian of his high school graduating class. After completing his studies at A.A. Wilson, Ross accepted a scholarship to Wilberforce University in Ohio, where he earned a degree in mathematics. He went on to earn a degree from the Philadelphia College of Pharmacy, in 1973. After completing his education, Ross accepted positions first at Dow Chemical and later at E.H. Robbins Pharmaceutical Company. During his 24 years at E.H. Robbins, he worked in research and development and in operations and production, where he was the manager of pharmacy. After leaving E.H. Robbins, he shifted his focus to community pharmacy, accepting both a paid position at a Richmond area CVS and a volunteer post at one of the city's free clinics, where he is currently the pharmacist in charge. Ross has also held leadership positions in regional pharmacy and healthcare organizations. From 1990 to 1996, he served on the Virginia Board of Health, an appointee of then Governor Douglas Wilder. His 9-year term on the State Board of Pharmacy spanned from 2002 to 2011. Ross has also held prominent posts in religious, fraternal, and academic organizations. A long-time member of Richmond's Ebenezer Baptist Church, he is the current Chairman of the Finance Stewardship Ministry for that institution. He is also a member of the Alumni Board of Directors for the Alumni Association of Wilberforce University, and he has served as State President and District Director of the Alpha Phi Alpha Fraternity, Inc. Ross has received many awards for his distinguished service to both his profession and his community, including the Alpha Phi Alpha National Alumni Brother of the

Year Award (in 1987), the 2009 Compassionate Care Award from the Richmond CrossOver Healthcare Ministry free clinic, and many others.

Dr. William Ross, Jr.: Educated in Malvern until his family relocated to Philadelphia, Pennsylvania at the start of his high school career, Dr. Ross earned his bachelor's degree at Central State University in Wilberforce, Ohio. He began his career as an educator when, after graduating from college, he became an elementary school teacher in the Philadelphia public school system. He advanced quickly and soon became Philadelphia's first African American school supervisor. He went on to serve as principal for several area schools, including George Brooks Elementary, Morton McMichael Elementary, and Wagner Junior High School. In addition, he served for 14 years as superintendent of the city's District One. Immediately prior to his retirement, Dr. Ross worked as the District Superintendent for Priority I Programs. In addition to his undergraduate degree, Dr. Ross holds a certificate of advanced study in urban education from Harvard University and a doctorate of education from the University of Sarasota. Dr. Ross has held a number of positions and memberships in community organizations, including the National Association of School Administrators, the Student Welfare Council, the NAACP, the Urban League, and the Mt. Pisgah A.M.E. Church of Philadelphia. He has served as the Eastern Regional Vice President for Alpha Phi Alpha Fraternity, Inc., the chairman of the Education Foundation of Alpha Phi Alpha, and the president of Alpha Phi Alpha's Rho Chapter.

Alice Marie Burks Stewart: A graduate of A.A. Wilson High School, the late Agnes Marie Burks Stewart was the first African American to earn a nursing degree from Indiana University at Kokomo, where she specialized in medical intensive care unit and cardiac care unit (MICU-CCU) nursing. She worked in the MICU-CCU field for a total of 28 years, 23 of which were spent at the John L. McClelland V.A. Hospital in Little Rock, Arkansas. In addition to her work as a critical care nurse, Stewart was also involved in parenting advocacy at the national level. In 1991 she became involved with the National Coalition of Title I/Chapter I Parents. She held a number of positions in the organization, including State Area Representative (for 3 years), Regional Steering Committee member (3 years), Pulaski County Special School District's Title I Parent Advisory Council (4 years), and National Board Member (6 years as State of Arkansas and Region VI National Representative). A daughter of the late Rev. W.C. Burks, Sr. and Nancy C. Glenn Caradine, Stewart joined the Greater New Hope Baptist Church in 1947, at the age of ten. A lifelong member of the church, she held a number of positions of authority and responsibility. As a youngster, she served as a Sunday school teacher, as the secretary of the Baptist Training Union, and as the assistant secretary of the Sunday school. After completing her college education, she returned to Malvern, where she served as the president of the Media Center Library, the Chair of the Pastor's Aide, and a member of the Senior Choir. An active member of Malvern area community organizations as well as a local politician, Stewart was a president of the Hot Spring Black Heritage Council, a member of the Ouachita River Park Commission, and a participant in the successful campaign for the listing of Bethel A.M.E. Church and Tuggle Elementary School on the National Register of Historic Places. She also served two terms as the Wrightsville, Arkansas Alderman (from 2002-2004 and from 2005 to 2007).

Matthew Walker, Jr.: The late Matthew Walker, Jr. was born in Malvern to Addie Lee McAdoo and Matthew Walker, Sr. Although he enjoyed a lucrative career in automobile and insurance sales, he is most widely remembered for his success as a Northwest Texas area radio personality. After graduating from A.A. Wilson High School, Walker relocated to Southern California where, in 1965, he enrolled at West L.A. Junior College. He would go on to complete two years of study there and to earn degrees from Career Academy of Los Angeles (in 1969) and the Don Martin School of Broadcasting (in 1971). After completing his education, he was offered a position at Tyler Broadcasting-KROZ/KZEY in Tyler, Texas. He began his career at the station as a disc jockey, but would go on to serve as its program director, sales manager and, eventually, general manager. During a year's leave of absence, from 1990-1991, Walker served as an announcer at KISX Radio, also in Tyler. Even as he was building his career in media, Walker was also developing a career in sales. Between 1991 and 2000, he worked for

Willingham Auto Sales, Mutual of Omaha, Golden State Mutual Life, and Columbian Mutual Life. In 1998, radio veteran Rick Reynolds called on Walker to assist him in starting radio station KBLZ. He worked in sales for the station and also as an announcer. In 2007, he retired from KBLZ, due to illness. In addition to his achievements in sales and radio (both on and off the microphone), Walker was also the creator of the Soul Town TV Show (during the early 1970s); and, with his wife, Deborah K. Browning Walker, he was the producer of the Matt Walker's Gospel Hour program (in the early 21st century), of which he was also the host. The first African American to do television and radio sales in Tyler and the first African American to host a black-oriented television show in that city, Walker was also an innovator outside of his work in the media. In 1975, he founded the Tyler, Texas Juneteenth Celebration and the accompanying Miss Juneteenth pageant. Matthew Walker, Jr. died on November 27, 2007.

Jewell "Pete" Willis, Jr.: A graduate of Malvern Colored High School, Willis was one of the original founders of the Malvern-Wilson reunions (with Lillian Beard). A former co-captain of the Leopards football squad, he has since used his leadership skills in the areas of politics and community service. He served as an Arkansas delegate to the Democratic National Convention in 2004, and he is a member of the West-central Arkansas Planning and Development District, Inc. Board of Directors. He is also a member of the Henson Benson Foundation Board of Directors and the principal administrator for the Malvern-Wilson Scholarship Fund. A long-time Democratic Party activist, Willis won his first election to the post of Hot Spring County District 1 Justice of the Peace in 1980. He has held that post for more than 30 years.

Given the relatively small size of Malvern's African American population (today the black inhabitants of the city number less than 3000), the graduates of its segregated school system are notable simply for the sheer number and variety of their accomplishments. When those high achievers who were educated in Malvern before integration are viewed alongside those who were educated at Malvern Senior High School after integration, a pattern of high academic and professional achievement among the community's African American graduates becomes clear. As Jewel Willis suggests in the following assessment of black Malvern's achievements, the quest for high academic and personal attainment seems to be endemic to the region:

> [F]rom our school and our town, we were fortunate enough to have four black young men to enter into the NFL. They played for the San Diego Chargers, Chicago Bears, and Kansas City ... And, we have several doctors and lawyers and judges. And, even before my time, we had dentists. We had black police, you know ... [And] right there in Malvern now, we got three young ladies who are in medical school ... We have federal judges and doctors and lawyers and dentists all over the country from Malvern.[187]

The descendants of Malvern Colored and A.A. Wilson alumni have continued the tradition of excellence established by their forbears; and though the high schools that their parents and grandparents held dear are long gone, that the black community's legacy of hard work and high achievement lives on is apparent in the number of African American educators, health care professionals, professional athletes, and community leaders who have graduated from Malvern Senior High School during the decades since integration. Like the listing of distinguished graduates of Malvern Colored and A.A. Wilson, the following roster of distinguished African American graduates of Malvern Senior High School represents only a sample of the many high-achieving descendants of Malvern Colored and Wilson alumni who have come out of this small west-central Arkansas community:

Isaac Davis: An All-State offensive and defensive player at Malvern Senior High School, Davis earned Third-Team All-American and First-Team All-SEC honors in both his junior- and senior-year seasons. He was drafted by the San Diego Chargers in the second round of the 1994 NFL Draft. Davis played for San Diego for six years and was a starter for the Chargers squad that won Super Bowl XXIX. After leaving the Chargers, Davis was briefly on the rosters of the Minnesota Vikings and the Oakland Raiders. Following his NFL career, he played briefly for the XFL. Today he serves as an assistant football coach at the Parkview Arts and Science Magnet High School in Little Rock, Arkansas.

Dr. Rodney Davis: Born in Malvern, Dr. Rodney Davis is a graduate of Malvern Senior High School. He went on to earn a bachelor's degree from Ouachita Baptist University in Arkadelphia before entering the University of Arkansas for Medical Sciences in Little Rock. He transferred to the Tulane University School of Medicine in New Orleans and graduated from that institution in 1982. After completing his residency at the Madigan Army Medical Center in Tacoma Washington, he completed a fellowship in urology at the University of Texas M.D. Anderson Cancer Center in Houston, Texas. For eleven years, Dr. Davis served on the faculty of Tulane University's Section of Urological Oncology. He was simultaneously the chief of Urology at the Veteran's Administration Medical Center in New Orleans. He held both positions until 2007, when he was recruited to Vanderbilt, Meharry, and the V.A. hospital system in Nashville, Tennessee. Dr. Davis is currently Professor and Chairman of the Department of Urology at the University of Arkansas for Medical Sciences. In addition, he holds a number of posts in national professional organizations. He is a fellow of the American College of Surgeons, a chairman of the American Urological Association (AUA) Guideline Panel for Microscopic Hematuria, a member of the AUA Advisory committee to the American College of Surgeons, and a director for the African Medical Research Foundation U.S. (AMREF). Several times a year, Dr. Davis travels to remote hospitals across the continent of Africa as part of the AMREF Flying Doctors Outreach Program. A U.S. Army Veteran, Dr. Davis has held a number of medical positions both on active duty and in the reserves, in the United States and abroad. In addition to the Madigan Army Medical Center, he has also served at the 47th Combat Support Hospital in the Persian Gulf in 1990-91 and at the Task Force 399th Hospital in Al Asad, Iraq, in 2007. Currently a Colonel in the Retired U.S. Army Reserves, he has won a number of military honors including the Army Meritorious Service Medal and the Global War on Terrorism Service Medal. Today, Dr. Davis is an internationally known specialist in minimally invasive techniques in the treatment of urologic malignancies.

Madre Hill: Born in Fort Bragg, North Carolina, Madre Hill relocated to Malvern as child. Early on, he established himself as a football standout, playing so effectively that local youth football officials established the "Madre Hill Rule," effectively prohibiting him from continuing to score touchdowns if he had already scored three times and his team led their opponents by 14 or more points. After establishing several state records in football at Malvern Senior High School, Hill went on to a distinguished career as a running back for the University of Arkansas Razorbacks. There he was named to the Arkansas Razorbacks All-Decade Team for the 1990s. A painting depicting him and offensive lineman Brandon Burlsworth hangs in the University's Broyles Athletic Center. Hill was selected by the Cleveland Browns as the first pick in the seventh round of the 1999 NFL draft. He went on to play for the San Diego Chargers, the Oakland Raiders, and the Berlin Thunder. In 2004, after leaving professional football, he accepted a post at the University of Arkansas as a graduate assistant to football coach Houston Nutt. He was hired in 2005 to serve as the running backs coach for the University of South Carolina, and in 2006 he became the running backs coach at Florida International University.

Nerissa Witherspoon Knight: The inaugural recipient of the Malvern-Wilson Alumni Scholarship, Knight began her career in broadcast journalism during her undergraduate years at the University of Memphis. During that time she worked first as an associate producer (for KATV) and later as a reporter (for KTHV), both in Little Rock. She has worked as an anchor and reporter in several markets throughout the U.S., including Little Rock, Arkansas; Pensacola, Florida; Boise, Idaho; Milwaukee, Wisconsin; Beaumont, Texas; and Los Angeles, California, where she hosted *Today in L.A. Weekend*. She is currently the national news anchor for the *Eye Opener* morning news show on KDAF-TV in Dallas, TX.

Dr. Yolanda Lawson: Born in Dallas, Texas, Dr. Yolanda Lawson graduated from Malvern Senior High School in 1989, earning academic honors. She then enrolled at Arkansas State University (ASU), where she was the recipient of a Strong-Turner Alumni Chapter Scholarship.

At ASU, Dr. Lawson was a member of the Black Student Association and Delta Sigma Theta Sorority, Inc. She also worked as a lab technician. A zoology major, Dr. Lawson earned her bachelor's degree in 1993. In 1997, she graduated from the University of Arkansas for Medical Sciences in Little Rock. As an intern, she was part of the first obstetrics and gynecology cohort at Morehouse School of Medicine in Atlanta, Georgia. She completed her residency at St. Johnson's Hospital and Medical Center in Detroit, Michigan and then returned to Dallas, the city of her birth, to join an OBGYN group practice. After four years, she opened her own private practice. In 2011, she opened her second practice, a boutique clinic located in a late 19th-century Victorian home that she restored and converted for this use. The second of two such homes that she has restored, Dr. Lawson won preservation awards from the city for each. She now sits on the Board of the City of Dallas Preservation Society. In addition to running her own practice, Dr. Lawson is an associate attending physician at Baylor University Medical Center and the medical director for a family pregnancy center affiliated with her church. She is also active in a number of professional groups. During medical school she became involved in the Student National Medical Association, an organization for African American medical students. She remains involved with that organization as a proctor. Dr. Lawson is a member of the American College of Obstetrics and Gynecology and the National Medical Association, for which she serves as the Dallas area vice-president and the regional secretary.

Dr. Misty Jones Nolen: Dr. Misty Nolen's academic promise was apparent during her high school career. At Malvern Senior High School, she accumulated an impressive record of honors and achievements. An outstanding student in the humanities as well as the sciences, she placed third in the Harry Singer Foundation Essay Contest during her senior year at Malvern. After a successful college career, she earned her medical degree from the University of Arkansas for Medical Sciences. A highly-rated pediatrician, she completed her internship and residency at Arkansas Children's Hospital. She now works in private practice and is affiliated with the Central Arkansas Pediatric Clinic in Benton.

Highly regarded for her caring and compassionate manner, she was a recipient of the 2012 Patient's Choice Award.

Tony Ollison: A high school teammate of NFL standout Keith Traylor, Ollison played for four years as a defensive tackle for the University of Arkansas, where he was a two-time starter in the Cotton Bowl (1989 and 1990). After college, Ollison played briefly for the San Antonio Riders of the World Football League. He went on to become the assistant strength and conditioning coach for the University of Arkansas and the University of Tennessee. In 2000 he was hired as strength and conditioning coach for the Dallas Cowboys, a position he held for eleven seasons. Today Ollison is the Arizona State University Sun Devils Senior Assistant Coach for Sports Performance, working primarily with the football team.

Bobbie Jean Bluford Smith: A graduate of Malvern Colored High School, Smith holds a bachelor's degree in elementary education from Arkansas Agricultural, Mechanical & Normal (AM&N) College (now the University of Arkansas, Pine Bluff). She also holds a master's degree in curriculum and instruction from the University of Wisconsin, Milwaukee, and a master's in education psychology from the University of Wisconsin, Madison. Smith retired in 1993, after a distinguished 31-year career as a teacher, curriculum coordinator, Chapter I coordinator, and assistant principal in the Milwaukee Public School system. After retiring, she served on the faculty of Milwaukee Area Technical College. Smith has been an active member of several local and national community organizations and institutions, including Zeta Phi Beta Sorority, Inc., for which she was the national director for necrology. She has served as a membership solicitor for the NAACP and is a member of the National Council of Negro Women. An active member of Milwaukee's Calvary Baptist Church, she has also served as an organist for another local church, Ellison Chapel A.M.E.

Keith Traylor: A two-time All-state, All-conference linebacker at Malvern High School, Traylor was named 1980s Player of the Decade by the Arkansas Democrat-Gazette. He remains second in the history of the state for tackles completed in a single season by a high school player. After playing for two seasons at Coffeyville Junior College in Kansas, Traylor transferred to the University of Central Oklahoma where his distinguished senior record of 79 tackles, five sacks, two interceptions, and two fumble recoveries earned him a place among the top 75 players and coaches in the history of the Lone Star Conference. He was drafted in the third round by the Denver Broncos and he was named to the 1991 all-rookie rosters of both Pro Football Weekly and Football Digest. As a professional football player, he has earned an impressive five Super Bowl rings, including two with the Broncos and three with the New England Patriots.

Michael Anthony Wilson: After graduating from Malvern Senior High School, Wilson earned an associate of science degree in surgical technology from the University of Arkansas for Medical Sciences (UAMS) College of Health Related Professions, a bachelor of arts in sociology (in 1997) from Henderson State University in Arkadelphia, and a bachelor of science in nursing (1998), also from Henderson State. Michael's education has enabled him to work in a number of healthcare-related sub-specialties, including surgical nursing, intensive care nursing, emergency nursing, correctional nursing, and healthcare administration. He has worked at a number of hospitals and clinics in the Los Angeles, California area.

The Malvern-Wilson Reunions

When Malvern and Wilson graduates assemble for their triennial reunions, they are gathering not only to reminisce about and express pride in their own schools and achievements, but to serve as a living bridge between the struggles and accomplishments of the past, the achievements of today, and their aspirations for the future. The alumni who gather for the Malvern-Wilson reunions offer material evidence of the infinite possibilities that await today's Malvern Senior High School students.

In 1981, Lillian Beard made the first series of calls soliciting alumni volunteers to plan and execute the first reunion event. She remembers that "Out of calling fifty or more people, only six met; Val Wright, Willie Carroll, Exie Carroll, Pete Willis, Marilyn Bailey," and Beard herself.[188] Jewell "Pete" Willis recalls that the reason the organizers of the first reunion came to call it "a homecoming" was in order "to encourage the greatest possible number of Malvern and Wilson alumni to return to the city in which they were raised." The messages that he and the early organizers of the event wanted to convey were, "Come on back home" and "come as you are."[189] Lillian Beard was particularly compelled by the idea that the reunion would provide an incentive for members of her immediate and extended family—especially her brother Titus Smith and her cousin Tom Green, Jr.—to visit Malvern on a regular basis.

High school reunions are notorious for the anxiety that they produce in possible attendees, especially those who fear that their activities since graduation might not display sufficient signs of success to their former peers and rivals. Jewell Willis and co-founder Lillian Beard initially addressed this possible obstacle to the Malvern-Wilson reunion events by conveying clearly and unequivocally that the welcome they extended to their fellow alumi was unconditional. The returning graduates come from all walks of life. They share the common experience of having attended one of Malvern's "colored" high schools, but in their post-graduate years, they have pursued many different paths. The returning alumni represent a range of economic classes, geographical regions, and education levels; and yet none of the differences are ever a source of friction or shame. Willis explains:

> We went out and did well. I'm proud of all of them. All of us didn't go to college. All us didn't get the master's and the Ph.D., but when we come home for the school reunion, we don't mention those things. We don't mention 2-room apartment against his 6 bedrooms. We don't mention that. He or she doesn't mention that. We just come back as a family, as friends, loved ones, and enjoy each other, and that's the way it should be.[190]

Not only do the reunions look past differences in class and achievement, they also smooth over any remaining conflicts rooted in the shifting tensions and loyalties of high school. Rather than fuel the flames of disagreements and rivalries from the distant past, the reunions have served as a cherished time for Malvern Colored and A.A. Wilson alumni to connect with those people who shaped many of the formative experiences in their lives. The first reunion set the tone for all subsequent gatherings. Dr. Samuel Benson remembers it as "an opportunity to first of all go back and see the people that you grew up with, the people who were around you."[191]

Lillian Beard and Jewell Willis first met to discuss the possibility of a joint reunion of Malvern Colored and A.A. Wilson alumni in 1981; but, Willis concedes, "we never did get anywhere in '81." In 1982, however, Beard and Willis began to move forward with their plans. The idea to begin the Malvern and Wilson reunions grew out of what Jewell Willis describes as an already occurring tradition throughout the South. "I think the reason we wanted to start," recalls Jewell Willis, "[is because] people used to come back home for every ... fourth of July."[192]

One of the organizers' first decisions was that theirs would be an all class reunion, bringing together all living graduates of both of Malvern's African American high schools. "Our classes were small—we're talking about class as [small] as 25 and 30," explains Willis, "so when you start saying class reunion, well, you're getting a very few people." Consequently, recalls Willis, since "1945 was the first year of senior class graduation from Malvern [Colored High School], we started [inviting] people from 1945 up to ... integration."[193] Lillian Beard remembers thinking that "a whole school reunion would be great and we could get everyone to come home at the same time."[194] The idea occurred to Lillian Beard and Jewell Willis that "if we [did] the reunion [in the summertime], not only will you see relatives, you will also see friends."[195]

Since 1982, Jewell Willis and the other reunion organizers have expanded the reunion to include Malvern Senior High School graduates and other family, friends and descendants of Malvern Colored and A.A. Wilson alums.[196] Today, the Malvern-Wilson alumni reunion has come to play an important role in the life of the greater Malvern and Perla community. The triennial gatherings have become something of an area institution, with portions of the proceeds from the reunions going back to the city in order to help maintain and support its residents. "We now have enough financing," explains Willis, "that when we get through paying [our expenses], we still have a little bit left over, so we can contribute some of the money to scholarships." "And," he continues, "sometimes our cemeteries are not well kept, [and] we go and get people to clean [them]."[197]

The reunions have also become quite a significant event for the area's tourism and hospitality industry, as this anecdote from Jewell Willis illustrates:

> One year we had so many people there, and they was renting cars out of Little Rock, and the man said, "well, what is going on in Malvern?" They said, "what you mean?" [He] said, "we are out of cars for rental." And then the small compact cars they was out of, and they started letting them have the large cars for the same price—just take them all. And Hertz and National [and] Budget, they just about ran out of cars.[198]

The first Malvern-Wilson reunion was held from August 12 through August 14 of 1983, the product of several months of hard work and organizing from a committed group of alumni volunteers. In addition to co-founders Lillian Beard (who was on the Souvenir Booklet Committee and also served as the Corresponding Secretary) and Jewell Willis (who also served on the Entertainment Committee) each of the following alums played a critical role in organizing the first of the Malvern-Wilson reunion weekend:

> Willie Carroll, Chairman of the first reunion and Chairperson of the Souvenir Booklet Committee.
>
> Marilyn S. Bailey, Recording Secretary and member of the Registration and Souvenir Booklet Committees.
>
> Herschel Smith, member of the Publicity, Registration, and Souvenir Booklet Committee.
>
> Sarah B. Smith, member of the Publicity and Souvenir Booklet Committees.
>
> Edward L. Green, member of the Publicity Committee.
>
> Val Wright, Jr., Treasurer and Picnic Chairperson.
>
> Exie J. Carroll, member of the Registration Committee.

Nearly 250 Malvern Colored and A.A. Wilson alumni, family and friends attended the first reunion. On the opening night, X.L. Jones was the master of ceremonies, Rev. Orestus D. Dismuke offered an invocation, and Willie J. Carroll gave the official greeting. Malvern Mayor Bill Scrimshire welcomed all of the assembled alumni and guests on behalf of the city, and Edward Green issued a welcome on behalf of Malvern's business community. Music on the opening night of that first all-class reunion was provided by Miss Valerie Womack (Miss Malvern of 1983), who sang a solo, and by the assembled Malvern and Wilson graduates, who closed out the evening's events with a rousing rendition of the school song.

Willie Carroll, the chair of the first Malvern-Wilson reunion, would continue to serve in that post until shortly before his death in 2001. He was succeeded in that post by Jewell "Pete" Willis. Under Willis's leadership, the reunions have retained all of the events that have come to define this three-day celebration. The event begins on Thursday evening with a gospel concert featuring choir members from the local churches. Friday evening includes a "get re-acquainted hour," followed by a short program of speeches and music. For the Malvern and Wilson graduates, the first evening is a bittersweet time for rekindling friendships and renewing acquaintances, but also for mourning those who have passed away during the years since the last homecoming. "[Every] three years," explains Willis, "there's always someone missing out of the puzzle—[due to] sickness or death. You can't ever get the whole crowd back every time."[199]

A highlight of the Friday evening program is the presentation of the Malvern-Wilson Alumni Scholarships. The funds are awarded to current Malvern Senior High School students who have shown academic promise. The scholarship grew out of reunion organizers' interest in adding a community service component to the homecoming celebration. "It was decided," explains Dr. Samuel Benson, "that we need[ed] to have some cause. We [could not] just get together to party; we got to have something else." To award current Malvern Senior High students with scholarships funded by Malvern and Wilson alumni is to put into action the values transmitted to Malvern Colored and A.A. Wilson alums during their own high school years. "[Our teachers] really made the point clear that education was the answer," recalls Dr. Benson, "and so, in a way, [the scholarships] are a tribute to so many important people—the Baileys, Essie Bullocks, the Harts, the Joneses, and just many, many—all the teachers." For Dr. Benson and other alumni, the scholarships are "clearly a way [to] carry on the tradition [of valuing education], to pay tribute to [their teachers], and carry on what was important, education."[200]

Applicants for the Malvern-Wilson Alumni Scholarship undergo a rigorous selection process. Recipients must confirm that they have been admitted to a college or university. A scholarship committee comprised of Malvern Colored and A.A. Wilson alumni reviews all applications. Winners' scholarship funds are sent to his or her institution, with funds applied directly to the students' accounts.[201] Award recipients receive funding throughout their academic careers. Willis notes that there are "some kids that we follow four to five to six years if they're going to be a doctor or lawyer." Say Willis, "we continue every year, as long as they fill out the application." Students who wish to continue to receive funding after their first year, however must annually provide the scholarship committee with a copy of their college grades. "We don't just send you the money just because," explains Willis. "We want to know what you're doing, [and] we follow up."[202]

The Malvern-Wilson reunion awarded its first scholarships in 1991. Initially the award was funded, as Jewell Willis explains, by the "monies left over after we had paid all our bills." The amounts were fairly modest. "[It] wasn't but $300 or $400 or $500, $600 per head," he recalls. In subsequent years, however, the size of the awards has "taken off," largely due to the generosity of alumni donors like Dr. Samuel Benson. With a larger pool of funding has come the ability to expand the reach of the scholarships. Now, "not only are we giving it to black kids," notes Jewell Willis, "we're giving it to white kids, also." The alumni have adopted this policy of race-blind giving because, says Willis, "we're trying to put all of this aside about race and everything, and we're just trying to have a fair shake across the board."[203]

That the alumni scholarships are awarded to students of all races and ethnicities underscores the commitment on the part of both the regional and national Malvern-Wilson alumni groups to serving the needs of the greater Malvern population. Dr. Benson emphasizes that "This is not a black club, this is an organization that's there to help the community, and we're very pleased ... that this scholarship is open to anyone." [204] This commitment to serving the needs of the entire greater Malvern community is also evident in the alumni group members' plans for expanding the scope of their outreach in the region. Dr. Benson hopes to expand the funding base for the Malvern-Wilson alumni scholarships through partnerships with the Acme Brick Company and other area businesses, with the goal that, in the coming years, the alumni organization "will be able to send anybody to college [who] wanted to go and ... who didn't have resources."[205]

The first Malvern Senior High School student to be awarded a Malvern-Wilson Alumni Scholarship was Nerissa Witherspoon Knight, in 1991. The Emmy award-nominated television news anchor and reporter remembers how important the scholarship was in helping her to reach her goals:

> [W]hen I applied for the Wilson Alumni Association scholarship, it was an opportunity to get that leg up, to get that help, to get the part and the piece that was missing. And though it wasn't all that was needed, it was a $1000 scholarship—it was just enough to bridge that gap between, say, Pell grant, tuition ... books, room, and board; and so it was a great help. [206]

Her experience as a recipient of the Malvern-Wilson Alumni Scholarship reinforced for Knight the importance of giving back to the community that had given so much to her. "When it came time to give back," says Knight, "I thought about what [the community] gave to me." Today she considers herself privileged to be a part of "that link—that chain" that connects each generation of students who graduate from high school in Malvern to the younger generations that will follow; and when the scholarship funds, alumni organizations, and schools need support, she does not hesitate to "write that check."[207]

Since Nerissa Witherspoon Knight, there have been 27 additional recipients of the Malvern-Wilson Alumni Scholarship. They are: Donnie Lewis, Brandie Cooper, Rodrick McGill, Andryea Reed, Alexis Huell, Keisha Hearn, Jonathan Carroll, Geremy Carroll, Henrietta Bailey, Kamario McAdoo, Jasmine Luster, Ty Napper, Taylor Regans, Grant Williams, Chelsea Long, Tanisha Bradford, Taiqura McNeely, Samuel Sanders, Cameron Rose, Whitney Jones, Appifany Wills, Parris Bryant, Gregory Johnson, Talesha Brim, Shakesha Smith, Kyle Hearn, and Vesha McNeely.

After Friday night's opening event, with its statements of welcome from local clergy, politicians, and business leaders and the awarding of the alumni scholarships, Malvern-Wilson reunion attendees begin their Saturday on a more informal note. On Saturday, the entire community gathers as the assembled Malvern-Wilson alumni participate in a parade down Main Street. The similarity between this procession and the homecoming parades of the past is not coincidental. Explains Jewell Willis, "[W]e try to find some of the ladies that were football queens thirty years ago, forty years ago, we get the convertibles and ride them through [town], and we get the school band."[208] Additional parade participants include the police department and at least one local fire truck, with the emergency vehicles adding their flashing lights and sirens to the sights and sounds of the day.

The parade is followed by block parties, at which reunion guests eat, chat, listen to music and, in the words of Jewell Willis, they "just have a good, good time."[209] The highlight of the Saturday activities is the reunion banquet, usually held at the historic Arlington Hotel in nearby Hot Springs. During the first reunion, this event was held at the Ramada Inn. "We didn't have any money to put [up] in advance," recalls Willis, but the Ramada Inn was willing to "take a chance on us."[210] The first reunion banquet, in 1983, was attended by nearly 250 guests. Since that time, the event has grown even larger, and recent reunions have attracted between 400 and 450 alumni, family members, and friends.[211]

If the Saturday evening banquet is the climax of each reunion, then the reunion address is the climax of the night. The assembled community gathers not only for food and fellowship, but to honor and enjoy the words of a distinguished guest speaker selected from the community of Malvern Colored High School, A.A. Wilson High School and, more recently, Malvern Senior High School alums. "[W]e always go back and get someone from the school, what we call high achievers ... the lawyers, the doctors, and the professional athletes," explains Jewell Willis. He emphasizes, however, that this focus on some of the most professionally accomplished alumni means, "No disrespect for the people that didn't go to college. We're not excluding them."[212] The banquet is followed by a dance, also held at the Arlington, which features live music and a spirited atmosphere of camaraderie and fun.

In 1983, Dr. Samuel Benson was chosen to deliver the very first Malvern-Wilson reunion address. In subsequent years, other distinguished Malvern Colored and A.A. Wilson graduates have served as the Saturday night speaker. The following is a partial list of the Malvern-Wilson reunion banquet speakers, in the order in which they spoke:

Dr. Samuel Benson, in 1983

Dr. Patricia L. Green Griffen, in 1985

Dr. William Ross, Jr., in 1988

Dr. Ted Carroll, in 1991

Mrs. Bobbie Jean Bluford Smith, in 1994

Mr. Harry Roberson, Jr., in 1997

Mrs. Nerissa Witherspoon Knight, in 2006

Hon. Raner C. Collins, in 2009

Dr. Samuel Benson, in 2012

On Sunday, the final day of the alumni weekend celebration, attendees gather at the city park for a picnic. Jewell Willis describes this, the closing event of the weekend, as a casual affair at which, "you've got your tie off and your flip flops on."[213] Participants make the most of this last opportunity to take pictures and enjoy food and drink with many of their most cherished friends and former schoolmates. The end of the picnic means that another Malvern-Wilson reunion has come to an end and, says Willis, "everybody starts crying again." An unspoken concern for many of the alumni guests is whether or not the classmates and friends who are at the current reunion will be able to return for the next. For Willis and the other attendees, "It's a big thing." Like many of those present, he cannot help but ask himself this question: "It's gonna be three more years [until the next reunion]. Will I be back [and] will I see you?"[214] He describes the scene at the close of the reunion festivities:

We hug, we kiss, we laugh, we cry, because we know that the group you got there then, you will not have the same group ever again, for whatever reason, sick or death or what[ever might happen] between those three years. And so we all say goodbye with a tear in the corner of our eye because we never know if we will ever meet again.[215]

Chapter V

Commerce, Commitment, and Community: Why Malvern's Black Schools Were Effective

"{W}e didn't just have middle-of-the-road teachers, we had the best."

—Jimmy Hunter, Wilson High
School, Class of 1966

When Malvern Colored and A.A. Wilson graduates are asked why their respective high schools were so very effective at preparing students for academic and professional success, virtually all will respond that the key to black education in Malvern and Perla was the extraordinary teaching staff, not only at the secondary schools, but at the elementary and middle school levels, as well. In its final chapter, this brief history of Malvern's African American school system and the community out of which it grew explores the reasons behind the startling and extraordinary accomplishments of its educational institutions, beginning with an examination of the effectiveness of the city's African American teachers, recounted in the words of former Malvern and Wilson students. The chapter goes on to examine the economic, social, and geographical factors that created the Malvern region as one in which black teachers were able to hone and practice their craft and black students were free to grow and develop as both citizens and scholars.

In the decades before integration, teaching at the primary and secondary levels was one of the few employment options open to college-educated black residents of the Malvern area. Considerably smaller than nearby

Hot Springs and with an industry-based economy, Malvern and Perla were able to accommodate only a limited number of physicians, attorneys, and scientists, and many black Malvern and Perla residents who desired, after finishing college, to make their home in the area entered the field of public education. Thus, in Malvern and Perla, as in many African American communities in the first half of the 20th century, teachers were culled from among the most academically talented students in the region. The high intellectual ability of Malvern's black teachers was a point of pride for Wilson High School alumnus Jimmy Hunter. "Something that I feel good about," he says, "is the people that came back here." "If you think about it," Hunter continues, "those people were the best of the best because ... if they wanted to stay here in this area, they had to come back and teach us." As a result, Hunter recalls, "We didn't have people [who] were just middle-of-the-road teachers, we had the best, before we integrated."[216]

The ability of Malvern's black public schools to attract intellectually gifted and academically accomplished teachers throughout the Jim Crow era was not only a reflection of the limited options available for black college graduates in the region, but also of the narrow range of occupations available for highly-educated black people in all parts of the U.S. "If you were going to contribute to your race and you were smart," explains Dr. Samuel Benson, "there weren't very many things open for you on Wall Street, so ... the smartest people of our community wound up being teachers." For Malvern's black schools, Dr. Benson adds, "that was an extremely important thing."[217]

Malvern's black teachers were not only highly educated and intellectually gifted but also deeply committed to the academic progress and overall well-being of their students. "They cared so much," recalls Jewell Willis.[218] Malvern teachers understood that the education of their students' minds was inextricably linked to the overall health of their bodies and their spirits. "All of our teachers were very stern," remembers Judy Pierce, "but they were good teachers, [and] they taught us ... the real way to play ball and ... how to take care of our bodies, and ... they gave us all the good things we needed ... for this life today."[219]

Like instructors at the college level, Malvern and Wilson teachers shared not only their own academic knowledge and expertise, but they also taught their students how to investigate and acquire knowledge for themselves. Laura Hunter remembers this as one of the aspects of her A.A. Wilson High

School education that best enabled her to move into the business world once integration began expanding opportunities for black men and women. For Laura Hunter, "[T]he plus side of having attended Wilson High School was that our teachers taught us how to do things." "We learned atomization of details," she explains, "but they [also] taught us how to learn." That her teachers believed deeply in each of their student's capacity for academic growth and success was but another benefit of attending Malvern's African American schools. Says Hunter, "Our teachers had [a] kind of belief in us. Telling us that we could do it and believing we could do it, that enabled us to do it."[220]

At Malvern's African American public schools, not only were teachers committed to their students' development, but the students also had greater access to their teachers. The small size of their classes facilitated plenty of individualized attention for boys and girls who needed it. Jimmy Hunter remembers the important role of small classes and frequent teacher contact: "We had that kind of instruction, that kind of attention, and that kind of push, and some people need that; and it worked out good for a lot of us." For Hunter, the high level of individualized instruction "is the missing ingredient today because of the numbers [of students]."[221]

The one-on-one interactions between teachers and students enabled Malvern's African American instructors to communicate clearly and unequivocally about their high expectations for each pupil's academic performance. "Being successful," explains Alvin Murdoch, "is something that the teachers in Tuggle and Wilson ... demanded of you." During his elementary school years, Murdoch's principal, Sophronia Tuggle," would give motivational speeches about once every week, and she would always talk about education." Murdoch still remembers the day when she advised her assembled students that education was a gift that would last a lifetime. Tuggle emphasized that, "Once you get it in your head, they can't take it from you."[222] Principal Tuggle's stern encouragement provided Murdoch with a strong foundation that served him for the rest of his school years and beyond; and because she was the head of Malvern's black elementary program, "That foundation was set early on." Murdoch's parents reinforced the messages and values that his teachers and his principal conveyed. Says Murdoch, "[That] foundation was really set through our parents, because a lot of our parents were taught by the same teachers. So, we knew when we went to school that [the teachers] were speaking as our parents."[223]

Jimmy Hunter attended school in Cleveland for part of his elementary and junior high years, and he remembers that the curriculum in his Ohio school was, in some respects, more advanced than in Malvern's African American public school system. "For example," he explains, "some of the classes that were not given in the eighth grade here [in Malvern] I had already had [previously] in Cleveland." Still, "the difference at Wilson was the ability of the teacher to see something in you and then make sure that it was going to come out of you." The small class sizes in Malvern were, he believes, one of the greatest assets of the city's black schools. In Malvern, explains Hunter, "It wasn't a situation where [the teacher] had too many kids to teach. They could give you that one-on-one [attention] if you needed it." The ability to provide individualized attention enabled Malvern's teachers to identify and nurture each student's special talents. "If you had abilities," recalls Hunter, "you weren't going to be able to keep it [a secret]. They were going to bring it out no matter what it took ... especially if you showed any kind of promise."[224]

Although Malvern's African American instructors held students at all levels to very high standards of performance, many students understood the transition out of elementary school—to Malvern Colored or A.A. Wilson—as a transition into even greater levels of academic accountability. Judy Pierce still remembers the feelings of uncertainty she experienced upon entering her first year at the junior/senior high school: "[F]irst of all, when I got into the seventh grade, we really had to learn." She felt "a little fear" at the thought of the new expectations that awaited her. "The fear," Pierce recalls, "was that you go to the big school, you have to get your lesson, [and] that's number one."[225]

Even though Malvern Colored and A.A. Wilson were relatively small high schools, the faculty and administration used their resources to create innovative programs that responded to the diverse interests and skill levels of their students. At A.A. Wilson, Jimmy Hunter was part of an experimental program of advanced courses. "There were seven boys and seven girls," he recalls. That virtually all of the participants have gone on to achieve success in their adult lives is a testimony to the effectiveness of this initiative. Says Hunter, "Those same people, they might not be rich or anything like that, but they have had successful careers or still have successful careers."[226]

When Dr. Samuel Benson was a student at Malvern Colored High School, there was no pilot program for advanced learners, but this did not prevent instructors from providing him with specialized coursework and individually designed curricula that nurtured his talents and gifts. For Dr. Benson, mathematics came easily and, noticing his aptitude in this subject, his teachers responded with customized assignments that allowed him to move forward at a pace that encouraged his growth in this area. He remembers that his teachers "would give [him] more complex problems" than were the standard for his grade level," noting that this approach "was obviously very helpful to me later on."[227]

At Malvern's African American schools, teachers did not, however, limit their individualized care and attention to those students who were the most academically gifted. Malvern Colored and A.A. Wilson alumni remember their teachers as deeply committed to instilling in every one of their students a sense of his or her own capacity to achieve. "If you were willing to learn," says Jimmy Hunter, "it was just wonderful"; but, he adds, "if you slacked off ... you didn't have to worry about your parents getting on you," the implication being that the teachers would step in and insure to you worked to your potential. Indeed, Hunter, who would go on to a rewarding career in California's telecommunications industry, attributes much of his success to his teachers' deep faith in their students' abilities. "I think they just wanted people to be successful," he explains, "and that was always the attitude—yes you can. It made a difference for me."[228]

Malvern's African American teachers were held in high regard throughout the community. "The hope of my great grandmother ... was that all of her kids were going to be teachers," recalls Dr. Samuel Benson, because, "At the time, there was ... no job that was considered higher or more important in the community except the ministers."[229] Yet, the respect accorded to the community's black teachers and principals was only one of the reasons for the strong and profound connection between the values, goals, and attitudes advanced in Malvern's African American public schools and the values, goals, and attitudes that the larger black community held up for itself and its children. Indeed, Malvern's black public schools were as much a part of the community as the students they served; and the teachers who educated these students were, themselves, the neighbors, friends, and congregation members who were served by the black community's other institutions—it's churches, businesses, and political and social organizations.

As a result, the ideas and ideals advocated in the classroom were reflected in all aspects of black life in the area, not only because the black parents and teachers of Malvern and Perla shared many of the same beliefs and goals, but also because students encountered their instructors in settings and events far beyond the classroom. Explains Henry Mitchell, "[E] ven though it was a school, it was really a community-based facility [and] when the school teachers—most of them—lived in your community, you saw them after you went home also."[230] Jimmy Hunter recalls that, "[M]y first grade teacher was my next door neighbor."[231] Teachers' proximity to their students, even beyond the classroom, expanded their sphere of influence to include their students' lives outside of school. "They had a lot of influence," recalls Alvin Murdoch, "because they were our Sunday school teachers, they were our neighborhood mentors." As a result, says Murdoch, "they really had full control of our basic education and molding our little lives."[232] Like Jimmy Hunter, Judy Pierce's family also lived next door to one of her teachers, and Mrs. Cooper held Pierce to the same standards of responsible behavior and comportment in their neighborhood as she did when they were together in the classroom. Judy Pierce recalls how her mother's relationship with this teacher functioned as a deterrent to any misbehavior at or around her home:

[W]e were real playful and so she told us we had to get our work, and we told her "yes ma'am we would," or she'd tell our mother, and that wasn't very good. Oh, if she told our mother that we didn't get our lesson, my mother would whoop us, and, you know, they believed in spanking children then … We didn't want mama to do that so we did what Mrs. Cooper said because she was right next door to us, and she would tell our mother.[233]

Alvin Murdoch sums up the relationship between Malvern's black teachers, their students, and the city's black population in the following description of the community relations that shaped his childhood learning experience:

[Y]ou heard the term, it takes a village? Well, that's what it was … Your whole surroundings were put into just a village concept because everybody lived in the neighborhood and the neighborhoods were where you learned and that turns into the schools. I mean your mom can stand on the front yard and talk to your teacher so there's no disconnecting there. Or they would see each other in church and they would discuss maybe you or some other business that's going on in the community. The teachers, your parents, the neighborhood, the schools, that was your life. And … basically you can ask anyone who lived in this area—the Malvern area—and probably any other area in the South; your neighborhood was your learning and your comfort zone.[234]

With so much support and attention from their teachers, their parents, and other adults in the local area (clergy, merchants, et cetera), the students in Malvern's African American schools felt loved and cared for, not only by their teachers and parents, but by the entire community. For Alvin Murdoch, the fact that teachers and parents worked together in shepherding the city's black children through their primary and secondary school experiences "made you feel secure," because "where[ever] you were at in your life … someone was there to nurture you, to admonish you, and to … tell you that you're part of something greater than you." Murdoch remembers how "The neighborhood—the village mentality—was [that] everybody was your child, and they were treated as such."[235] Mrs. Henrietta Bailey was especially generous in her efforts to support her students outside of school hours. She was even willing to work with students in her home. Jewell Willis recalls that, "You could go to her house and things that you didn't understand or get, she was very patient with us, because she knew how valuable it was to pursue an education."[236]

In Malvern and Perla, both teachers and parents alike understood the necessity of education. In shaping their approach to education, many teachers drew on the role it had played in their own lives. For many of the African American parents in the area, however, the commitment to educating their children came from a distinctly different place. "The reason why it was so important [to these parents]," explains Jewell Willis, "[was] because over half of them … didn't have the opportunity." And, like many of his peers, his parents' passionate investment in educating their child was a key motivating factor in his own academic performance. "Our parents knew … that [education] was what we need," recalls Willis, "and we didn't want to disappoint them." [237]

One of the primary avenues through which Malvern's African American parents were able to support their local schools was the Parent Teacher Association (PTA), that met one or two times per month.[238] Many parents also supported the schools by reinforcing at home the same academic standards to which the teachers held their children in the classroom. Like many other parents in the community, Frances Calhoun upheld the values and priorities of her child's teachers by prioritizing high intellectual achievement in the home. In the following anecdote, she shares an example of how she maintained high academic standards and an atmosphere of accountability for her son, Dr. Samuel Benson:

> [E]very month or every six weeks, they'd send me what he'd made, you know. So one time I got his [report] card … It wasn't no A and it wasn't no B. It was a C. And I called him. I said "What is that?" He said "Oh, that." I said "Uh-huh. That." He said "Well, see, them other kids [were] chewing gum and all that stuff. And I don't carry [no gum]." I said "I'll give you a box of chewing gum to carry. But you better not never come up here with that kind of score." I said, "I would like to have some As. But don't come up here with no Bs … It's just the less [gum] you going to get [from me]. He said "Yes, ma'am" … the next time I saw that boy's report card…all I could see was As, As, As.[239]

Mrs. Calhoun's educational standards and aspirations for her son extended well beyond his high school years, as exemplified in the following episode: "He told me once that he wanted to go in the Army. And I said no. He told me once that he wanted to work in the brickyard. And I said, 'No, I don't want you handling bricks. I want a pencil in your hand.'"[240]

The deeply committed and highly skilled instructors, the strong parent/teacher/community relationships, and the high academic standards to which both teachers and parents held the region's black children goes a long way toward explaining why, over the course of only 23 years, Malvern's African American high schools graduated such a lengthy roster of young men and women who would go on to achieve extraordinary success in their adult lives. It is, however, impossible to fully account for the unusual effectiveness of this small, semi-rural, segregated school district without a thorough exploration of the role of the region's economic and racial climate in creating an environment in which African American upward mobility could develop without provoking the type of racist violence and suppression that devastated so many communities in the Jim Crow South.

A critical factor contributing to the ability of Malvern's African American schools to achieve such extraordinary results was the city's capacity to attract and retain both a cadre of highly skilled and educated schoolteachers and a stable population of lower-middle to upper-middle-class black families. Malvern was able to attract and retain these populations for the following reason: because its strong industrial base eliminated the often bloody competition between blacks and whites for economic and social standing that plagued much of the South; because of its healthy and supportive climate for African American businesses; because of its proximity to major transportation and shipping routes; and because of its unique relationship to the city of Hot Springs, Arkansas, a national and international tourist destination. The unusual effectiveness of Malvern area black schools only truly becomes comprehensible through an examination of the ways that the complex interaction between access to transportation, proximity to Hot Springs, plentiful employment, thriving black businesses, and a stable African American middle class helped shape an environment in which black achievement (economic and intellectual) was able to flower.

To begin to understand the role of the region's racial and economic conditions in creating and sustaining effective black schools, it is useful to return to the 1940s, when Malvern's African American community gained its first high school program and graduated its first class of high school seniors. Malvern's black community made important educational advances in the 1940s, advances that highlight the difference between the racial climate that Malvern's black community was experiencing at the time and the racial climate that prevailed in the rest of the state. For example, the important political strides made by Malvern's black residents during the Jim Crow era is perhaps best represented by the 1949 election of Rev. L.R. Williams to the Malvern City Council. This transformative moment in the relationship of Malvern's African American community to the local city government contrasts sharply with state government efforts to limit the individual freedom of blacks during the very same period. In 1947, just two years before Malvern's voters elected the first African American to serve on their city council, the state legislature in Little Rock passed laws instituting the following segregationist measures:

- Mandatory segregation at polling places, on motor carriers, in railroad cars, and within prisons.
- Mandatory separate restrooms in mines.
- A poll tax.
- The designation of sexual relations between blacks and whites as illegal.
- The creation of separate tuberculosis hospitals for black people.
- Mandatory segregation in public schools.

That African Americans were making political advances in Malvern at the very same time that the state legislature was advocating for *decreased* autonomy, equality, and political power for black people highlights the diffe-rence between the relatively tolerant relations between the black and white communities of Malvern and the more acrimonious relations between these groups in other parts of Arkansas.

School spending in segregation-era Malvern also reflected the divide between the racial climate in the west central region of Arkansas (where Malvern is located) and the racial climate in the rest of the state. This is highlighted in a 1955 study of education spending in a representative sampling of Arkansas counties, completed in the wake of the Brown v. Board of Education Supreme Court decision. Although the study, which appeared in the *Journal of Negro Education*, does not include the specific statistics for Hot Spring County (where Malvern is located), it is clear that during the year leading up to the historic Brown v. Board decision, adjacent Garland County (in which the city of Hot Springs is located) had some of the highest per pupil spending in the state for black students. In the 1953-54 school year, the per-pupil spending for Garland County public school enrollees was $143 for white students and $146 for black students. Of the four counties in which spending for black students was slightly higher than it was for white students, three of them were located in the western portion of the state (Garland, Washington, and Sebastian counties). All of the counties in the study that presented with the lowest expenditures for black students were in the far eastern portion of the state. There are: Crittenden, with $65 per black student and $151 per white student; Phillips, with $86 per black student and $137 per white student; Lee, with $67 per black student and $163 per white student; St. Francis, with $81 per black student and $150 per white student; Chicot, with $84 per black student and $167 per white student; Lincoln, with $88 per black student and $165 per white student; Jefferson, with $95 per black student and $141 per white student; and Ashley, with $93 per black student and $158 for each white student.[241] The disparity between per pupil school expenditures for black students in select counties in west-central Arkansas and the per pupil school expenditures for black students in other parts of the state—especially the cotton- and rice-growing regions of eastern Arkansas—reflects a historic divide between the more hospitable racial climate that defined the African American experience in Malvern and surrounding communities, and the more tenuous relationship of black people to economic and political self-determination in other regions of the state.

The fact that race relations in pre-integration era Malvern and Perla were considerably less strained than in other parts of Arkansas is largely attributable to two factors. One is the availability of plentiful non-agricultural employment for black and white laborers alike, from the late 19th century onward. Another is its accessibility, enhanced by the presence of the railroad as well as by Malvern's proximity to the city of Hot Springs, whose tourist industry not only provided an additional and nearby source of non-agricultural labor (thus expanding the base for an even larger black middle-class community), but also drew a wide range of visitors from across the U.S. and beyond, all of whom had to pass through Malvern in order to reach the popular spa destination. As a result, neither Malvern nor its residents were impoverished or isolated, factors that created an atmosphere in which African American upward mobility could take place without provoking the type of violent backlash against black prosperity to which isolation and poverty often gave rise (in communities like Elaine, Arkansas as well as in other southern communities, like Rosewood, Florida and Tulsa, Oklahoma). Hot Springs historian Orval Albritton experienced Jim Crow segregation from the position of a young man in the racial majority. He remembers west-central Arkansas as, "a soft spot in the South," in terms of its racial attitudes. "Now," he explains, "the theaters here, they were segregated, the ball games were segregated, and the schools were segregated," but, "we were tolerant."[242]

In this way, Malvern resembled many of those larger coastal cities more commonly associated with African American upward mobility in the period before integration. Indeed, one of the reasons Malvern's African American schools were able to provide their students with the kind of individualized academic attention and college preparatory curricula that were (and, to a great extent, still are) available almost exclusively to privileged students in major metropolitan areas of the county is that, even during the earliest decades of the 20th century, long before the successes of the civil rights movement, the city enjoyed a diversity of employment options and a level of accessibility to other parts of the state and the nation that were rare in all but those larger urban population centers (New Orleans, Atlanta, Philadelphia, New York, Washington, D.C.) more commonly associated with African American political, educational, and economic opportunity. Not only did prosperous black communities like these demand access to high-quality education for their children, but they also produced a steady supply of highly-educated black men and women well-qualified to staff African American schools.

With a population of black workers who were able to earn a steady and consistent income, Malvern was also able to provide African Americans with another important source of economic opportunity that has, across time and across regions, been an important stepping stone to upward mobility, and that is business ownership. Jewell Willis recalls that during his school years in Malvern, the city's black community sustained, "several barbershops, beauty shops, and ... several small grocery stores." The African American business owners of Malvern and Perla owned a variety of establishments, including grocery and dry goods shops run by Mr. Chick Ross, Miss Morgan, Miss Clay, Mr. Bryant, and Miss Vanilla. There were also some unique niche businesses like Paul's Egg Store, Mr. Littleton's dentist office and watch repair, and Uncle Sam's, which sold candy, gum, and other items.[243]

Gerald Jordan's great uncle, Shag Miller, owned a general store. Jewell Willis's childhood memories of the establishment are of its generous size and its wide range not only of grocery items, but also of adult beverages. "Mr. Shag Miller [was] right on the highway," recalls Willis. "He had a huge grocery store, [and] he sold beer—he had a beer license." Jordan's and his mother's experience with the general store provide an excellent example of how the economic opportunities in Malvern and Perla did, for a time, help stave off and even reverse the tide of that "Great Migration" that was drawing so many black people in other regions of Arkansas and the South away from their home communities. In a 2005 interview printed in the Arkansas Democrat, Jordan tells the story of his family's departure from and—shortly after—their return to Malvern:

> [I]t would have been 1949 because I was nine months old when my family moved to Kansas City, and that became my Kansas City connection there. We lived there until I was about ten years old, and my great uncle, who was really more like my grandfather because he and his wife reared my mother, retired from his general store business because of his illness. He developed adult onset diabetes and just decided he couldn't handle the store anymore with what he needed to do to take care of himself, so he asked my mother who was, in effect, their only child, to come back and take over the store. So we moved back to Arkansas in 1960, I guess it was.[244]

Jordan remembers the "measure of financial independence" that business ownership provided. As a result, observes Jordan, "my upbringing was little different from someone who grew up in a family [in]—say—eastern Arkansas, where they were beholden to a big farm, and you were working just a share of it." Explains Jordan, "we weren't rich by any stretch of the imagination; we were certainly comfortable; but, in retrospect, I can see that that afforded all of us ... a measure of independence that probably did not exist throughout the South for African Americans."[245]

Another popular black business in Malvern was the store owned by Eutah and Viola Jones. Located at the corner of Page Street and Oak, Jones's establishment housed a store, a dry cleaning and delivery service, gasoline pumps, and a café; and, like Shag Miller, the Joneses held a beer license that enabled them to sell alcoholic beverages. Although it was not a dry town, even during the 1940s and '50s, there were no liquor stores within the city limits, and so businesses like those owned by Shag Miller and the Joneses had a near monopoly on a portion of the local market.[246]

While most of the industrial jobs in Malvern employed only men, small businesses provided an avenue for women to establish a degree of financial independence. Alvin Murdoch describes the gender-based division of labor in pre-civil rights era Malvern and Perla:

The men had jobs. If it wasn't at Acme Brick, it was at Reynolds metal company, and your mom would do domestic work and just maybe take in some work on the side. There weren't a lot of opportunities for women ... during the '50's, unless they would be a teacher or they would have to leave to be a nurse or something in that order. There weren't a lot of opportunities for women—especially black women—during that period of time. A notable exception was the business work.[247]

Some of Malvern's black businesses were run by women either on their own or with their spouses, as exemplified by Eutah and Viola Jones and Mr. and Mrs. Shag Miller. Some women, however, were the sole proprietors of their establishments, a position that afforded both autonomy and the potential for financial security.

For several decades, Frances Calhoun, the granddaughter of Taylor Henson, owned a beloved and thriving store on Highway 67 in Perla. The daughter of Hezekiah and Nettie Henson and the granddaughter of Taylor Henson, she inherited her family's penchant for real estate and business ownership. Her son, Dr. Samuel Benson, remembers Mrs. Calhoun as "a great business woman" who purchased her first piece of land at the age of 17.[248] She describes the events surrounding that purchase:

> Somebody came along and said "Where's your daddy?" I said "Oh, he's around by the potato cellar I guess." He said "Well, I had some good bargain to sell some land. But I know you wouldn't be able to buy it." I said "How you know? I ain't got no glass pockets. How you know what I could do?"[249]

Mrs. Calhoun began her business on a very small scale. Her son, Dr. Samuel Benson, recalls that, at first, "She carried fish that she had bought out to Perla in my little red wagon, and sold fish out of that wagon." From selling those fish, she "saved enough money so that [she and her son] could move in and [buy] half of Old Man Tyler's store."[250] With the proceeds from her first business, she was able to buy out Tyler's establishment and move herself and her young son into the attached apartment. Mrs. Calhoun was a tireless store owner who worked long hours at times when many stores might have remained closed. "I used to go to church every Sunday," she recalls, "and then I would come back and pull off my little [church] clothes, put on a uniform, and go to [work] selling gas and stuff."[251]

Mrs. Frances Calhoun opened her second store in a building that her father built for her near the Acme Brick factory in Perla. The store that he built had living quarters in the rear. Both of Mrs. Calhoun's stores prospered, and their combined profit enabled her to build a house beside her Perla establishment. In addition to building a new home for herself and her son, her businesses also afforded her some moderate luxuries. Dr. Benson recalls that his mother "used to always have a new automobile."[252]

Dr. Benson recalls that, like other aspects of this small, Arkansas community, shopping in Malvern was not as thoroughly segregated as in other parts of the South. This was reflected in the diversity of his mother's clientele. She had white customers as well as black, and she extended credit to people of all races, as did many white grocers in the area. Recently renovated to serve as a museum and community meeting hall for the residents of Malvern and Perla and their guests, Mrs. Frances Calhoun's shop served as a gathering place throughout its time as a local establishment. Larry Parker remembers that Mrs. Calhoun was always ready with a fun or fascinating story to share. "I used to stop in the store there," he recalls, and "I would get an ice cream sandwich or a coke and sit there and talk with her and just listen to her."[253]

Given the involvement of the city's black women in running its African American shops, it should come as no surprise that one of the most successful businesses in the history of Malvern's African American community was owned by a black woman. Tillie Yancy Benson Graham, paternal grandmother of Malvern Colored High School alum Dr. Samuel Benson, owned a funeral parlor that served the area's African American community. The story of how Dr. Benson's grandmother became so successful in what was, at the time, a male-dominated profession begins like so many Malvern stories, with migration away from a poorer farming region to the more prosperous and industry-based economy of the Malvern area. Dr. Benson describes Graham's unusual path to her position as the area's most successful black funeral director:

> My grandmother ... got married to George Benson. And George was a carpenter and also a smart businessman and he convinced her with her little small son, my father, to go to Eckels in Philadelphia, a

highly regarded professional school that I understand is still in business, that teaches people to become morticians. So she finished up at Eckels, came back, and they started a small business in Wabbaseka, Arkansas; but they didn't like it because it was primarily a farm community and people were poor. They worked as sharecroppers and that sort of thing. But she somehow or George somehow heard about Malvern and so they came to Malvern and they were highly successful there. She started her own burial association which, of course, is like an insurance company. I'm not sure you have to have an insurance license for it, but it was a burial association where people could pay 25 cents a month or something like that, or if it was a dollar but I am sure it was less, like 25 [cents]. And that would then allow you to have a [funeral]. It would be in the church. It would be one that a person would be satisfied with ... Families seemed to be pleased.[254]

Tillie Yancy Benson Graham was the first African American woman mortician in the state of Arkansas. Not only was Mrs. T.Y.B. Graham an important force in shaping the economic life of the area's black community, but she was also a critical influence in the life of her grandson, young Samuel Benson. A prosperous businesswoman, she was able to afford comforts and indulgences rarely experienced by her black Malvern neighbors. Jewell Willis recalls her as the first black person he ever saw driving a Packard, one of the most coveted luxury automobiles of the first half of the 20th century.

Graham's taste for the trappings of luxury had a powerful impact on her beloved grandson. Her luxury items were not indulgences acquired through inheritance or through the doting benevolence of a wealthy husband. Rather, all of the extravagances in which she partook came as a result of her hard work as a funeral director and her husband's hard work as her coffin maker and business partner. Recall's Dr. Benson, "She was extremely important in the sense that she gave me my champagne tastes. In order to be able to have champagne you must be successful at whatever it is you want to do." It was his early exposure to fine clothing and automobiles that instilled in him a desire to create a lifestyle in which he too could have access to the settings and privileges of a prosperous life. Says Dr. Benson, "I recall having my first tailored suit when I was 6 years old, and I recall riding around with her in the car that she used in her business, which was a Packard or a Cadillac or one of those. So early I got to see that part of the world."[255] The presence, in this small, Jim Crow-era community, of an affluent black woman entrepreneur illustrated to the young black boys and girls in the local area that anything could be achieved or acquired through education and hard work.

Mrs. Graham, like other similarly successful area business owners, played a role in state and local politics. She was part of a handful of community leaders with whom the governor would meet during each election season. Dr. Benson recalls her involvement with the state gubernatorial campaigns:

> [E]very four years, when the governor was going to be elected, or every two years—whatever it was—he would come down and visit all the important black and white folks in Malvern. That would include the business people like my grandmother, Eutah Jones, Shag Miller and others ... But it also included the white people who were business people ... and so forth."[256]

The prosperity of Malvern and Perla was evident not only in the array of jobs available and the variety of black-owned business that were established during the years before WWII but also in the growth and proliferation of the city's black churches. Churches were direct beneficiaries of the region's black prosperity. Dr. Samuel Benson explains: "In order to [have thriving black churches], you needed people who were supporters, people who had money ... so there was sufficient black business people to be able to fund adequately the churches and the schools."[257]

In the years prior to integration, Malvern was home to nine African American churches, all of which are still in operation. They are:

- First Missionary Baptist Church, Malvern (founded in 1877, under the leadership of Rev. Balm Whitlow and Rev. John Davis).
- Greater New Hope Missionary Baptist Church, Malvern (founded in 1865, under the leadership of the Rev. Balm Whitlow).
- New Director Missionary Baptist Church, Perla (founded during the late 19th century by Rev. Balm Whitlow, Deacon Chatman Williams, and Sister Amy Lee).

- Mount Willow Missionary Baptist Church, Malvern (founded during the 1870s, under the leadership of Rev. Balm Whitlow).
- West End Church of God in Christ, Malvern (founded at the turn of the last century, under the leadership of Elder D.W. Welch).
- Bethel A.M.E. Church, Malvern (founded as St. Luke African Methodist Episcopal Church in 1884, under the leadership of Rev. W.M. Stewart).
- Mount Zion Missionary Baptist Church, Malvern (founded in 1914 by Rev. R.S. Bowers).
- East End Church of God in Christ, Malvern (founded by Elder and Sister Oscar Glenn).
- First Missionary Baptist Church, Rockport (founded under the leadership of Rev. R.S. Shorty).

These churches played an integral role in the lives of Malvern area black residents, providing fellowship, community outreach, and a moral center for their membership. Moreover, the black church was, in the words of Dr. Samuel Benson, "a leader in terms of social issues," throughout the South.[258]

The relationship between Malvern residents' access to plentiful jobs in the industrial sector and the ability of its African American community to sustain a number of thriving churches and businesses is clear: without stable employment there would be no sizeable population of African American shoppers to form a solid customer base for the area's black entrepreneurs who, in turn, were able to provide a strong foundation of economic support for its religious institutions.

The region's strong economy owed much to its unique geology and its fortunate geography, which gifted the region with a vast supply of clay for brick making, bauxite for aluminum processing, and a thickly forested landscape well-suited for logging and milling. Rich enough in natural resources to support three industries, Malvern, Hot Springs, and other communities in west-central Arkansas were built on terrain that was as inhospitable to the state's largest cash crops (cotton and rice) as it was suited to the growth of an industrially-based wage labor economy. The natural resources that defined the Malvern and Hot Springs region gave rise to a fourth industry that contributed significantly to the second major factor in the area's relatively tolerant racial climate, its accessibility to other parts of the state and the nation. Rural and isolated, eastern Arkansas towns like Elaine and St. Charles and counties like Crittenden, Jefferson and Lonoke saw the greatest proportion of the state's racial violence, including the Elaine riots of 1919 (in which more than 100 African Americans are estimated to have been killed in a horrific massacre) and the St. Charles lynchings of 1904 (in which 13 African Americans met their end).[259]

In contrast to these rural, isolated east Arkansas counties and towns, Malvern was not only easily accessible due to its function as a major railway hub, but it also drew large numbers of visitors from all over the nation because of its unique position as the gateway to the nearby resort city of Hot Springs. With its naturally occurring warm mineral waters, Hot Springs was the home of a spa industry that attracted guests from across the U.S. and beyond. "[T]housands of people from all over the world each year came to Hot Springs for the healing waters," explains Dr. Samuel Benson; and, during the period when railroad travel was the primary means of passenger transport, "they had to come through Malvern because the Ouachita mountain range kept them from going [directly] to Hot Springs." The popularity of Hot Springs brought a steady influx of urban vacationers through what would otherwise have been an isolated industrial burg, and "the trains that were going from St. Louis to New Orleans or St. Louis to Dallas all came through Malvern; so people from Chicago and New York and so forth who were coming by train would get off at Malvern."[260]

Not only did the regular stream of out-of-state visitors stave off the type of provincialism that afflicted so many of Arkansas' more isolated communities, it also provided a level of notoriety for Malvern. As early as the 1880s, Malvern began drawing the attention of major publications like *Harper's Magazine* and the *Christian Recorder*. In 1888, *Harper's* mentioned the city of Malvern in a description of the Diamond Jo railroad:

[Hot Springs] is fifty-five miles southwest of Little Rock, but to reach it the traveler must leave the Iron Mountain and Southern Railroad at Malvern for a ride over a branch line of some twenty miles. Unfortunately, this is a narrow gauge road, and however ill a person may be, a change of cars must be made at Malvern.[261]

The April 14, 1881 issue of the *Christian Recorder* includes a brief article in which Rev. Israel Derricks makes explicit the role of the Diamond Jo railroad in cementing the close relationship between Hot Springs and Malvern. He writes:

> Hot Springs is a city of 5,000 inhabitants, having streets, railroad, gas works, steam fire engines, churches of all the various denominations, the usual places of amusement and all the other attractions incident to a large watering place. The city is reached by a railroad, which connects with the St. Louis, Iron Mountain and Southern Railroad at Malvern, a point about forty miles south of Little Rock. The distance from Malvern to Hot Springs is about twenty-two miles. The Hot Springs railroad makes close connection with the two daily trains on the St. Louis, Iron Mountain Southern Railroad, and conveys their passengers in comfortable cars on an easy-going ride from Malvern to Hot Springs in about one hour and a half.[262]

Not only was Malvern a gateway to other population centers, but its easy access via rail made it something of a destination in and of itself. In 1916, the State Baptist Conference selected Malvern as the site of its 63rd Anniversary Gathering. The roster of speakers included ministers from four different states, including "Pres. L.R. Scarborough, D.D., of Fort Worth, Tex, J. H. Eager, D.D., who represented Baltimore, Maryland, and New York, N.Y., and Rev. C.F. Tiemann, of Stafford, KS."[263] Malvern's distinguished visitors were not, however, limited to members of the clergy. On June 10, 1936, the city received a visit from what may well have been the most prominent guest in its history. On that day, President Franklin Roosevelt and First Lady Eleanor Roosevelt traveled by car from the city of Hot Springs to tour Rockport and Malvern. After dining at the Lake Catherine home of Arkansas telecommunications and energy magnate Harvey Couch, the Roosevelts participated in welcoming ceremonies in Rockport and Malvern, before traveling by train from Malvern to Little Rock.[264]

Malvern's proximity to Hot Springs became the foundation of an intimate relationship that was beneficial to both cities, and that connection remains in place to this day. Hot Springs, Arkansas could be described as sharing all of the positive qualities of Malvern, but on an amplified scale. As in Malvern and Perla, there are plentiful non-agricultural jobs for people of all races and ethnicities. While Malvern's natural resources provided ample employment opportunities in heavy industry, Hot Springs' most valuable resource, its 47 naturally heated mineral springs, provided ample work in a tourist industry that, even in the era before the civil rights movement, attracted and accommodated black guests as well as white. Beginning in the late 19th century, black and white visitors to the city were served by spa, hotel, and restaurant staff of all ethnicities. In "Old Buck," a sketch written in 1942 and republished in 2007, African American poet and scholar Sterling A. Brown quotes the title figure, an aging black Hot Springs resident, on the topic of race relations among employees of and visitors to the city's attractions. In the following excerpt, Brown's title character describes the racial climate of the South's preeminent spa city:

> Because of government supervision of the bath houses, Buck explained, Hot Springs is a piece of the North set down in the heart of Arkansas. Big shot whites and Negroes from all over the country come there; there is a racing season for thirty days every year and money gushes like the springs. After his apprenticeship, Buck preferred to work at the remaining Negro bath house: "An old time Negro can work in the white places."[265]

Among the "Big shot ... Negroes" who Old Buck and other black residents might have encountered in Hot Springs were the pastors and bishops of the A.M.E. Church, who regularly held both regional and national conventions there, beginning in the early 1870s. The historic Visitors Chapel A.M.E. Church was built in Hot Springs in 1870 and almost immediately began to draw large numbers of black worshippers. The church also became a favorite destination for black religious and secular organizations seeking an appealing conference site. In 1876, the A.M.E. State Sunday School Convention based its operations at the Visitors Chapel; and in 1895, the College of Hot Springs held its first commencement exercises in its sanctuary.[266] A number of church dignitaries attended this event, traveling from cities and towns across the nation. Among the most distinguished guests were Professor Mungo Melanchthon Ponton of Boston University, an educator and clergyman who began his educational career at Yale University and would eventually go on to earn a bachelor's degree from Boston University, a master's degree from Lincoln University, and a Doctor of Sacred Theology degree from Morris Brown College.[267]

Other important national events that took place in Hot Springs include: the Conference of Southern Negro Educators, held in 1954; the 1909 meeting of the Annual Conference on General Health Conditions of Negroes in Southern States; the National Negro Business League Conference in 1923; and the National Baptist Convention (which held its annual and semi-annual gatherings at Hot Springs several times during the Jim Crow era).

In addition to service and professional organizations, Hot Springs was a regular stop for the national tours of many of the country's most popular African American performers, throughout the Jim Crow era. Jewell Willis remembers how his uncle, George Reed, would contact him and "He would say, 'Duke Ellington and them's gonna be in Hot Springs tonight,' or Count Basie, Cab Calloway … Earl Hines and all these large bands … Nat King Cole, Coleman Hawkins, Lester Young, and all these bands." While many of the concert venues in Hot Springs insisted on segregated performances throughout the Jim Crow era, black musicians of the period always made time to play additional shows specifically for their African American fans. Willis recalls how the touring musicians "would have to play the first set for the whites, [but] after the whites leave, [they] would go on and get down and have the 'black time,' so to speak."[268]

The city of Hot Springs did not merely tolerate black tourism, it welcomed and encouraged it. African American entrepreneurs funded the construction of hotels, bathhouses, and spas that served the black tourist market. These included the Pythian Hotel and Bathhouse, the National Baptist Sanitarium, the Crystal Bathhouse, the Crittenden Hotel, McKenzie's Motel, the Barabin Villa, and the Claridy House, among others. During the 1950s, while much of the South was experiencing an increase in internal tension and terroristic violence due to the rise of the Civil Rights Movement, Hot Springs remained a relative oasis as it continued to welcome African Americans guests from across the nation. Photo essayists Ray and Steven Hanley describe one of the city's efforts to attract greater numbers of black vacationers, published on the eve of the Brown v. Board of Education decision:

> The weekly *Hot Springs Visitors Bulletin* in 1953 carried a separate "Negro Section" of ads for businesses in this area. A joint ad was

sponsored by the National Baptist Sanitarium ... and the Pythian Hotel ... The ad proclaimed, "We extend an invitation to the Negro population of the United States to come to Hot Springs."[269]

Among the black visitors who took advantage of Hot Springs' openness to African American tourism were the residents of Malvern and Perla. Malvern offered Hot Springs a steady stream of revenue in the form of a nearby source of short-term visitors seeking to patronize its diverse spa and entertainment offerings. In exchange, Hot Springs provided Malvern with additional job opportunities and recreational activities. Malvern's Jewell Willis describes how employment opportunities in Hot Springs led to close ties between the African American communities in the two neighboring cities:

> Hot Springs has always been connected to Malvern in one way or another, even from economics to work, the work force and all. Some of the ladies would go over to the hotels, and, you know, if they couldn't find two jobs in Malvern that suited them, they could go to Hot Springs in the clubs and work doing odd jobs and drive back and forth—commute, you know—from Hot Springs to Malvern. And, Hot Springs [has] just really been a brother or sister city to Malvern. And we just knew so many people in Hot Springs and when I was in the work force, Reynolds Aluminum Company was located between Malvern and Hot Springs ... I knew so many guys from Hot Springs and them from Malvern, so we would socialize, you know and we'd go over there. It was just a lot of friends, lot of friends from Hot Springs.[270]

Like Malvern, Hot Springs was home to a number of black-owned businesses. In addition to hotels and spas, African American entrepreneurs owned restaurants, stores, doctors' offices, law offices, and even gambling halls. Malvern and Perla residents would travel to the city to enjoy dining, shopping, and entertainment experiences or to obtain medical and legal services beyond what was available in their own community, and many have fond memories of childhood trips to the city. Malvern Avenue was the heart of the black community in Hot Springs, and many Malvern residents paid regular visits to that bustling district. Jewell Willis shares this recollection of a childhood trip to Malvern Avenue:

[M]y dad had this A model [Ford], and we had to go from Malvern to Hot Springs by what they call Cook's Mountain. It was paved. But sometimes our car, you had to shift down in low gear and crawl over the mountain. It wasn't a steep mountain, you know, but the cars didn't have much power ... [Hot Springs] was very exciting to me and my sister, you know, four or five times larger than Malvern. And, we would go to Aunt Katy and Uncle Pete, we called 'em. Uncle Pete (that was his name) he was a hundred and some years old when he passed away; but, anyway, they would show us around the black-owned stores and clubs and bathhouses.[271]

In this brief remembrance, Willis calls attention to a key component in the relationship between Malvern and Hot Springs, the difficult terrain that had to be crossed to reach the resort city. In the years prior to air and automobile travel, the mountainous overland the larger city relied on its smaller neighbor, situated adjacent to but not fully within the Ouachita mountain range, to serve as a rail and stagecoach hub where travelers could rest and prepare for the last leg of their trip.

The number of successful black business owners in their own home-town insured that Malvern's African American youth never had to wonder whether prosperity and financial security was possible for black people. For many young African American residents of Malvern, however, Hot Springs provided their first contact with black people of great wealth. For Jewell Willis, the urban affluence that he encountered in Hot Springs left a lasting impression. He shares this memory of encountering a wealthy black tourist during a family visit to the Hot Springs area:

Guys was coming from Dallas and Houston, you know, a lot of black guys who had a lot of money, and we could see they was driving Packards and Cadillacs and Buicks. They would have chauffeurs and they would have sacks delivered with money. And their chauffeurs and bodyguards, when they'd be gambling, they'd just reach in and get a handful and count it out. And, didn't nobody bother them, 'cause they was in a safe haven in Hot Springs.

Another source of wealth for Hot Springs, and one that contributed to the generally cordial relations between black and white residents throughout the region, was organized crime. From the 1890s through the mid-1900s, Hot Springs served as a regional hub for the underground economy, with English, Irish, Jewish, and Italian mobsters from the Midwest and the Northeast directing the city's lucrative gambling, prostitution, and bootleg liquor trades. Crime history aficionados point to the presence of Al Capone at various periods throughout the 1930s as an indicator of Hot Springs' important role in national crime syndicates that thrived before the end of World War II. Capone's armored car remains on display in the vast lobby of Hot Springs' historic Arlington Hotel, where it serves as a reminder of the days when Owney Madden, the Manhattan-born "English godfather," ran the Hotel Arkansas Casino and Al Capone, Lucky Luciano, Frank Costello, and Bugs Moran treated this scenic spa city as their semi-private retreat. Indeed, the popular characterization of Hot Springs as "Vegas before Vegas" refers to its Jazz-era role as the gangsters' vacation destination of choice. Says Robert Raines, the founder and director of the Hot Springs-based Gangster Museum of America, the city was "the only location where almost every bank robber, every underworld figure … was on their best behavior." Still, Raines reminds us, vacation or not, the nation's most prominent organized crime figures were wanted men, if not by the federal government, then by their rivals; and the location of the city, in the heart of the Ouachita mountains, was as appealing to its mob clientele as the restorative qualities of its waters. Explains Raines, "there was one way in, there was one way out," and for the gangsters of the era, that provided a measure of comfort.[272]

In addition to their efficient management of the so-called "sin" trades, whose revenue was an important part of the Hot Springs economy, the area's organized crime lords also brought to west-central Arkansas a racial sensibility that, while far from progressive in the contemporary sense, was considerably more broadminded than the extreme segregationism that was prevalent in the southern and eastern portions of the state. More interested in building their fortunes than in enforcing a particular racial dispensation, Capone, Madden, Costello, and others tolerated a level of interaction between African American and white city residents that was unusual for the time. There was, for example, some contact between black and white tourists in a small number of the city's spas. In addition, both Negro League and white professional baseball teams would travel to Hot Springs for spring training, where they would periodically square off against each other on the playing field.

Hot Springs' reputation as an outlier in the area of segregation in public accommodations dates back at least to 1903, when it was one of only three Arkansas cities in which the African American community protested the Streetcar Segregation Act, introduced by state representative Reid Gantt of—ironically enough—Hot Springs. Later the same year, when State Senator Joseph C. Pinnix escalated the segregation debate by proposing a bill that would have moved beyond segregation within the streetcars to propose an entirely separate system of cars for black people, the state legislators from Hot Springs were among the most vocal opponents of this measure.[273]

In the end, the most accurate term to describe the racial climate in Hot Springs, Malvern, Perla and surrounding communities (like Hope and Rockport) might be *laissez faire* or, in the words of Dr. Samuel Benson, "live and let live."[274] Although Hot Springs, Malvern, and Perla all experienced segregation in public accommodations (including schools) throughout the Jim Crow era, the racial climate in the region was generally tolerant and respectful, if not of the idea of full equality and integration, then at least of the notion that all had a right to pursue and enjoy a modicum of domestic comfort, financial security, and freedom from violence. Jewell Willis points out that although some white residents of outlying areas might occasionally have threatened and harassed black residents of the region, "they was minor incidents, [and] the police was right on it."[275]

While racial violence was an accepted part of the landscape in some parts of Arkansas, there was virtually no active hate-based terrorism in Malvern or Perla. "[W]e never had no race riots, nor anything of that nature that I can recall," observes Jewell Willis.[276] Charlie Carroll affirms Willis's assessment, noting that, in Malvern, "[B]lack and white have always … got along fairly well."[277] As early as the first decades after the end of Reconstruction, the Malvern region was noted to have less activity from white supremacist groups than in other parts of the South. In a 1930s Works Progress Administration interview conducted by his son, Samuel, former Malvern area slave Anthony Taylor recalls that "Where we was, the Ku Klux [Klan] never did bother anybody."[278]

While the prosperity of the local region, with its multiple industries and thriving businesses, was a significant contributor to the less antagonistic racial climate in Malvern and surrounding communities, the relationship between economic stability and a mood of racial tolerance was not unidirectional. In fact, the robust economy of the Malvern area (including the resort city of Hot Springs) was one of the reasons that white people in the area rejected the influence of the Klan and other racist groups. Actions taken by such groups had the capacity to destabilize the economy in ways that would undermine the fortunes of white and black residents, alike. Jewell Willis is unequivocal on this point, noting that, relative to the contempt and harassment experienced by African Americans in much of the segregated South, Malvern's black people "[would] be treated different because of economics."[279] It was, in short, in the best interest of Malvern's white business owners, city administrators, and law enforcement officials to maintain racial stability in their community.

Despite the understanding by Malvern's white residents that a degree of racial tolerance was critical to maintaining the economic stability of the city, segregation was a regular part of the daily practice of business there, throughout the Jim Crow era. The white-owned establishments of Main Street welcomed customers of all ethnicities, but when African Americans patronized those shops, there were certain conventions that were conscientiously observed. Jewell Willis recalls being taught that "if [you] were sent to town by our parents, you went exactly for that specific item, [and] if it's for the drugstore you [were] going to the druggist, [getting] the prescription filled, [and] you turn around and come out." Even outside the stores, Jim Crow conventions prevailed. Willis recalls, for example, that on weekends, "both sides of Main Street would be pretty well filled up with white shoppers from Malvern and its surrounding communities, and if they came [toward you], you just had to step off ... and let them pass."[280]

As Jewell Willis's recollections illustrate, Malvern was not a racial utopia. No southern community was fully immune to the practices and biases of the segregation era. Still, the prevailing understanding in Malvern and Perla that the economic fortunes of the black and white populations in the area were deeply intertwined was the foundation on which the region's prosperity was based. And it was because of the prosperity of the region that Malvern's extraordinary African American high schools were able to thrive and grow. Ironically, it was the success of those schools, more than any other single factor, that would eventually lead to a significant migration of Malvern's African American graduates to other parts of the country.

While many cities and counties throughout the South saw increasing levels of African American migration to the North throughout the first decades of the 20th century, Malvern's strong industrial employment base staved off significant African American out migration until the period after World War II. If Malvern graduated its first class of African American high school seniors in 1945, just a few months before the end of the war, then it also sent its first high school diploma holders to college in the same year. Greater numbers of black Malvern residents entering college meant greater numbers of young black men and women leaving the city, with only a portion choosing to return, once their schooling was complete.

Thus, the story of the Malvern-Wilson legacy is not only the story of teachers, parents, and communities joined together to insure opportunities for their youth. It is impossible to fully assess the impact of the area's black schools without taking into account the changes wrought by migration and loss. Still, in terms of the now familiar narrative of black migration—from racism and poverty in the South to greater tolerance and opportunity in the North—the Malvern-Wilson story deviates from the expected narrative. While books like James Baldwin's autobiographical novel *Go Tell It on the Mountain* and Richard Wright's *Black Boy* portray black northern migration as necessitated by the poor prospects for work, education, and safety in the Jim Crow South, black residents of Malvern, Perla, Hot Springs, and other west-central Arkansas communities had access to all of these components of a stable life. This very stability produced a school system that produced a generation of young black men and women whose educational preparation positioned them for career paths that Malvern's logging and manufacturing economy simply could not accommodate. Consequently, when Malvern's sons and daughters relocated to the greater Los Angeles and San Francisco Bay Areas, Chicago, Atlanta, and other large metropolitan hubs, most were seeking not greater comfort and safety, but greater access to a broader range of employment opportunities in the white-collar professions.

And yet the story of the Malvern Colored and Agnes A. Wilson high schools, their alumni, and the communities that fostered them is, in the end, less about migration from the area than it is about return. More critical to understanding the significance of the city's African American school system than the departure of its graduates is their faithful return—every three years, for the last three decades—to remember, to reflect on, and to celebrate the schools and the teachers that played such a vital role in shaping the men and women they would become.

Notes

Introduction

[1] Malvern and neighboring Perla, Arkansas are both located in Hot Spring County, a municipality adjacent to but distinct from Garland County, in which the city of Hot Springs is located.

[2] See Morrison, Toni, 32.

[3] For a semi-autobiographical account of one family's Northern migration, see Baldwin, James. *Go Tell It on the Mountain.* For a history of the Great Migration and it's aftermath, see Wilkerson, Isabel. *The Warmth of Other Suns. The Epic Story of America's Great Migration.*

Chapter I

[4] Patterson, Ruth Polk, xi-xii.

[5] Miles, Lendora Williams, 8.

[6] Benson, Dr. Samuel, January 2010.

[7] Taylor, Warren.

[8] *Slave Narratives: A Folk History of Slavery in the United States from Interviews with Former Slaves, Arkansas Narrative, Part 6,* 27.

[9] Miles, Lendora Williams. 8.

[10] *A History of the North-Western Editorial Excursion to Arkansas: A Short Sketch of Its Inception and the Routes Traveled Over, the Vies of the Editorial Visitors to Arkansas, as Expressed in their Paper,* 81.

[11] Capace, Nancy, 253.

[12] *National Newspaper Directory and Gazetteer,* 31.

[13] "Malvern...the Early Years," 5.

[14] Murdoch, Alvin.

[15] Hunter, Jimmy.

[16] Jasper, Marva.

[17] Jasper, Marva.

[18] Hunter, Laura.

[19] Benson, Dr. Samuel, July 2011.

[20] Hanley, Ray and Steven, 73.

[21] Smith, Kenneth L, 235.

[22] Parker, Larry.

[23] Parker, Larry.

[24] Bryant, Samuel.

[25] Green, Ed.

[26] Green, Ed.

[27] Hunter, Laura.

[28] Parker, Larry.

[29] Hanley Ray and Steven, 8.

[30] Green, Ed.

[31] Green, Ed.

[32] Green, Ed.

[33] Green, Ed.

[34] Pierce, Judy.

[35] "Brick Industry," *The Encyclopedia of Arkansas History & Culture.*

[36] Calhoun, Frances.

[37] Benson, Dr. Samuel, 2011.

[38] Woods, J.B., 15-17.

[39] Benson, Dr. Samuel, 2011.

[40] Benson, Dr. Samuel, 2011.

[41] Willis, Jewell "Pete," Jr., 2010.

[42] Green, Ed

[43] Willis, Jewell "Pete," Jr., 2010.

[44] Green, Ed.

[45] Willis, Jewell "Pete," Jr., 2010.

[46] Willis, Jewell "Pete," Jr., 2010.

[47] Willis, Jewell "Pete," Jr., 2010.

[48] Benson, Dr. Samuel.

Chapter II

[49] Davis, Ronald. L.F.

[50] The Arkansas Survey Report, 13.

[51] Graves, John William, 421-448.

[52] Graves, John William, 438.

[53] "Close of the First Term of the College of Hot Springs Last Night," 1.

[54] Perry, M.R., 93.

[55] "Helping the Negro Teacher in Arkansas," 375-6.

[56] Megna-Wallace, Joanne, 66.

[57] "Origins at Tuskegee." *National Trust for Historic Preservation.*

[58] "State Listings for Arkansas." *National Register of Historic Places.*

[59] Willis, Jewell "Pete," Jr., 2010.

[60] Jordan, Gerald.

[61] Hunter, Laura.

[62] Willis, Jewell "Pete," Jr., 2010.

[63] Willis, Jewell "Pete," Jr., 2010.

[64] Murdoch, Alvin.

[65] Hunter, Laura.

[66] Murdoch, Alvin.

[67] Pierce, Judy.

[68] Murdoch, Alvin.

[69] Jasper, Marva.

[70] Beard, Lillian.

[71] Beard, Lillian.

[72] Hunter, Laura.

[73] Hunter, Laura.

[74] Hunter, Jimmy.

[75] Hill, John.

[76] Murdoch, Alvin.

[77] Pierce, Judy.

[78] Murdoch, Alvin.

[79] Beard, Lillian

[80] Hunter, Laura.

[81] Pierce, Judy.

[82] Willis, Jewell "Pete," Jr., 2010.

[83] Willis, Jewell "Pete," Jr., 2010.

[84] Willis, Jewell "Pete," Jr., 2010.

[85] Willis, Jewell "Pete," Jr., 2010.

[86] Hunter, Laura.

[87] Willis, Jewell "Pete," Jr., 2010.

Chapter III

[88] Willis, Jewell "Pete," Jr., 2010.

[89] Willis, Jewell "Pete," Jr., 2010.

[90] Willis, Jewell "Pete," Jr., 2010.

[91] Benson, Dr. Samuel, 2011.

[92] Benson, Dr. Samuel, 2011.

[93] Willis, Jewell "Pete," Jr., 2011.

[94] Willis, Jewell "Pete," Jr., 2011.

[95] Willis, Jewell "Pete," Jr., 2011.

[96] Willis, Jewell "Pete," Jr., 2011.

[97] Beard, Lillian.

[98] Willis, Jewell "Pete," Jr., 2011.

[99] Willis, Jewell "Pete," Jr., 2011.

[100] Willis, Jewell "Pete," Jr., 2011.

[101] Beard, Lillian.

[102] Willis, Jewell "Pete," Jr., 2011.

[103] Willis, Jewell "Pete," Jr., 2011.

[104] Willis, Jewell "Pete," Jr., 2011.

[105] Willis, Jewell "Pete," Jr. 2011.

[106] Willis, Jewell "Pete," Jr., 2011.

[107] Willis, Jewell "Pete," Jr., 2011.

[108] Willis, Jewell "Pete," Jr. In this portion of his interview Willis adds the following aside: "I'm still using the work 'colored,' but that's the way it was."

[109] Benson, Dr. Samuel, 2011.

[110] Bryant, Twin Mary Bell, 91.

[111] *About Our People: The Black History of Malvern*, 56.

[112] Jordan, Gerald, 2010.

[113] Bryant, Samuel.

[114] Murdoch, Alvin.

[115] Pierce, Judy.

[116] Pierce, Judy.

[117] Bryant, Samuel.

[118] Murdoch, Alvin.

[119] Murdoch, Alvin.

[120] Hunter, Laura.

[121] Hunter, Laura.

[122] Hunter, Laura.

[123] Mitchell, Rev. Henry.

[124] Mitchell, Rev. Henry.

[125] Pierce, Judy.

[126] Bryant, Samuel.

[127] Hunter, Laura.

[128] Hunter, Laura.

[129] Hill, John.

[130] Mitchell, Rev. Henry.

[131] Hunter, Laura.

[132] Hunter, Laura.

[133]   Hunter, Laura.

[134]   Hill, John.

[135]   Hill, John.

[136]   Hunter, Laura.

[137]   Hunter, Laura.

[138]   Hunter, Laura.

[139]   Pierce, Judy.

[140]   Mitchell, Rev. Henry.

[141]   Hill, John.

[142]   Hill, John.

[143]   Murdoch, Alvin.

[144]   Pierce, Judy.

[145]   Hill, John.

[146]   Hill, John.

[147]   Hill, John.

[148]   Hill, John.

[149]   Bryant, Samuel.

[150]   Bryant, Samuel.

[151]   Murdoch, Alvin.

[152]   Jordan, Gerald, 2010.

[153]   Hunter, Jimmy.

[154]   Bryant, Samuel.

[155]   Bryant, Samuel.

[156]   Hunter, Jimmy.

[157]   Pierce, Judy.

[158]   Mitchell, Rev. Henry.

[159]   Bryant, Samuel.

[160]   Hill, John.

[161]   Bryant, Samuel.

[162]   Hill, John.

[163]   Hunter, Jimmy.

[164]   Sullivan, Geraldine.

[165]   Benson, Dr. Samuel, 2011.

[166]   Mitchell, Rev. Henry.

[167]   Hunter, Laura.

Chapter IV

[168] Murdoch, Alvin.

[169] Murdoch, Alvin.

[170] Murdoch, Alvin.

[171] Murdoch, Alvin.

[172] Murdoch, Alvin.

[173] Murdoch, Alvin.

[174] Pierce, Judy.

[175] Mitchell, Rev. Henry.

[176] Pierce, Judy.

[177] Hill, John.

[178] Pierce, Judy.

[179] Hill, John.

[180] Hill, John.

[181] Hill, John.

[182] Hill, John.

[183] Hill, John.

[184] Pierce, Judy.

[185] Pierce, Judy.

[186] Pierce, Judy.

[187] Willis, Jewell "Pete," Jr., 2010.

[188] Beard, Lillian, August 2009.

[188] Willis, Jewell "Pete," Jr., 2010.

[189] Willis, Jewell "Pete," Jr., 2010.

[190] Willis, Jewell "Pete," Jr., 2010.

[191] Benson, Dr. Samuel., 2011.

[192] Willis, Jewell "Pete," Jr., 2010.

[193] Willis, Jewell "Pete," Jr., 2010.

[194] Beard, Lillian, 2009

[195] Willis, Jewell "Pete," Jr., 2010.

[196] Willis, Jewell "Pete," Jr., 2010.

[197] Willis, Jewell "Pete," Jr., 2010.

[198] Willis, Jewell "Pete," Jr., 2010.

[199] Willis, Jewell "Pete," Jr., 2010.

[200] Benson, Dr. Samuel, 2011.

[201] Willis, Jewell "Pete," Jr., 2011.

[202] Willis, Jewell "Pete," Jr., 2011.

[203] Willis, Jewell "Pete," Jr., 2011.

204 Benson, Dr. Samuel, 2011.

205 Benson, Dr. Samuel, 2011.

206 Knight, Nerissa Witherspoon.

207 Knight, Nerissa Witherspoon.

208 Willis, Jewell "Pete," Jr., 2011.

209 Willis, Jewell "Pete," Jr., 2011.

210 Willis, Jewell "Pete," Jr., 2011

211 The reunion banquet with the heaviest attendance attracted 500 guests.

212 Willis, Jewell "Pete," Jr., 2011.

213 Willis, Jewell "Pete," Jr., 2011.

214 Willis, Jewell "Pete," Jr., 2011.

215 Willis, Jewell "Pete," Jr., 2011.

Chapter V

216 Hunter, Jimmy.

217 Benson, Dr. Samuel, 2011.

218 Willis, Jewell "Pete," Jr., 2011.

219 Pierce, Judy.

220 Hunter, Laura.

221 Hunter, Jimmy.

222 Murdoch, Alvin.

223 Murdoch, Alvin.

224 Hunter, Jimmy.

225 Pierce, Judy.

226 Hunter, Jimmy.

227 Benson, Dr. Samuel, July 2010.

228 Hunter, Jimmy.

229 Benson, Dr. Samuel, 2011.

230 Mitchell, Rev. Henry.

231 Hunter, Jimmy.

232 Murdoch, Alvin.

233 Pierce, Judy.

234 Murdoch, Alvin.

235 Murdoch, Alvin.

236 Willis, Jewell "Pete," Jr., 2011.

237 Willis, Jewell "Pete," Jr., 2011.

238 Willis, Jewell "Pete," Jr., 2011.

239 Calhoun, Frances.

240 Calhoun, Frances.

241 Hicks, Charles A., 175.

242 Albritton, Orvall.

243 Willis, Jewell "Pete," Jr., 2010.

244 Jordan, Gerald, 2005.

245 Jordan, Gerald, 2010.

246 Willis, Jewell "Pete," Jr., 2010.

247 Murdoch, Alvin.

248 Calhoun, Frances.

249 Calhoun, Frances.

250 "Dedication of Frances Hall." *Malvern Daily Record.*

251 Calhoun, Frances.

252 Calhoun, Frances.

253 Parker, Larry.

254 Benson, Dr. Samuel, 2011.

255 Benson, Dr. Samuel, 2011.

256 Benson, Dr. Samuel, 2011.

257 Benson, Dr. Samuel. 2010.

258 Benson, Dr. Samuel, 2011.

259 Stockley, Griff, 6-7.

260 Benson, Dr. Samuel, 2011.

261 Warner, Charles Dudley, 557.

262 Derricks, Rev. Israel, 1

263 *The American Baptist Year-Book*, 43.

264 "Hot Springs County," *The Encyclopedia of Arkansas History & Culture.*

265 Brown, Sterling, 43.

266 "Close of the First Term of the College of Hot Springs Last Night," 1.

267 Hamilton, Green Polonius, 117-120.

268 Willis, Jewell "Pete," Jr., 2010.

269 Hanley, Ray and Steven Hanley, 125.

270 Willis, Jewell "Pete," Jr., 2010.

271 Willis, Jewell "Pete," Jr., 2010.

272 Raines, Robert. Interview by Foster Braun. *American Road Trip Talk Podcast.*

273 Graves, John William, 441-2.

274 Benson, Dr. Samuel, 2010.

275 Willis, Jewell, "Pete," Jr., 2010.

276 Willis, Jewell, "Pete," Jr., 2010.

277 Carroll, Charlie.

[278] Taylor, Anthony.

[279] Willis, Jewell "Pete," Jr., 2011.

[280] Willis, Jewell "Pete," Jr., 2011.

Bibliography

A History of the North-Western Editorial Excursion to Arkansas: A Short Sketch of Its Inception and the Routes Traveled Over, the Vies of the Editorial Visitors to Arkansas, as Expressed in their Papers. Little Rock: T.B Mills & Co, 1876.

Albritton, Orval. Interview by Ajuan Mance. February 2010. Audio transcript.

Baldwin, James. *Go Tell It on the Mountain.* New York: Dial Press, 2000.

Beard, Lillian. "A History of the Malvern/Wilson Reunion" *The Malvern-Wilson Reunion: Welcome Home, Where It All Began, '26 Years' and Still on the Right Track.* Malvern: Malvern-Wilson Alumni, August 2009.

—. Interview by Pam Uzzell. April 2011. Audio transcript.

Benson, Dr. Samuel. Interview by Pam Uzzell. July 2011. Audio transcript.

—. Interview by Ajuan Mance. July 2010. Audio transcript.

—. Personal interview. 19 January 2010.

"Brick Industry." *The Encyclopedia of Arkansas History & Culture.* Web. 12 August 2010.

Brown, Sterling. "Old Buck," *A Negro Looks at the South.* Ed. Mark A. Sanders and John Edgar Tidwell. New York: Oxford UP, 2007. 37-50.

Bryant, Samuel. Interview by Pam Uzzell. December 2010. Audio transcript.

Bryant, Twin Mary Bell. "First Colored Majorettes: 1948-1950." *About Our People: The Black History of Malvern*. Malvern: Greater New Hope Baptist Church, 2000. 91.

Calhoun, Frances. Interview by Pam Uzzell and Dr. Samuel Benson. April 2011. Audio transcript.

Carroll, Charlie. Interview by Pam Uzzell. April 2011. Audio Transcript.

Carroll, Exie. Interview by Pam Uzzell. April 2011. Audio Transcript.

Capace, Nancy. *Encyclopedia of Arkansas*. Hamburg: North American Book Dist LLC, 1998.

"Close of the First Term of the College of Hot Springs Last Night." *The Christian Recorder Magazine* 30 May 1895: 1.

Davis, Ronald L.F. "Creating Jim Crow: In Depth Essay," *The History of Jim Crow*. N.p. N.d. Web. 18 August 2010.

"Dedication of Frances Hall." *Malvern Daily Record*. April 2011.

Derricks, Rev. Israel. "Hot Springs: The Waters and Their Properties—Diseases Especially Benefitted—Inebriety—Bath House Charges—Medical Fees—Potash Sulphur Springs—Diseases Cured or Benefitted—The A.M.E. Church's Location, &c." *The Christian Recorder Magazine*. 14 April 1881: 1.

Graves, John William, "Jim Crow in Arkansas: A Reconsideration of Urban Race Relations in the Post-Reconstruction South." *The Journal of Southern History*, 55.3 (1989), 421-448.

Green, Ed. Interview by Pam Uzzell. April 2011. Audio transcript.

Hamilton, Green Polonius. *Beacon Lights of the Race,* E.H. Clarke & Brother, 1911.

Hanley, Ray and Steven. *Images of America: Malvern*. Mount Pleasant: Arcadia, 2010.

"Helping the Negro Teacher in Arkansas," *The Southern Workman*, 42.7 (July 1913), 375-6.

Hicks, Charles. A. and A. Stephan Stephan. "Integration and Segregation in Arkansas--One Year Afterward." *The Journal of Negro Education* 24.3 (Summer 1955): 172-187.

Hill, John. Interview by Pam Uzzell. December 2010. Audio transcript.

"Hot Springs County," *The Encyclopedia of Arkansas History & Culture*. Central Arkansas Library System. May 2006. Web. 1 June 2010.

Hunter, Jimmy. Interview by Pam Uzzell. December 2010. Audio transcript.

Hunter, Laura. Interview by Pam Uzzell. December 2010. Audio transcript.

Jasper, Marva. Interview by Pam Uzzell. December 2012. Audio transcript.

Jordan, Gerald. Interview by Pam Uzzell. December 2010. Audio transcript.

Jordan, Gerald. Interview by George Arnold. *The Arkansas Democrat Project*. Pryor Center. University of Arkansas. 5 May 2005. PDF.

Knight, Nerissa Witherspoon. Interview by Pam Uzzell. June 2011. Audio transcript.

"Malvern...the Early Years." *About Our People: The Black History of Malvern*. Malvern: Greater New Hope Baptist Church, 2000. 3-5.

Megna-Wallace. Joanne. *Understanding I Know Why the Caged Bird Sings: A Student Casebook to Issues, Sources, and Historical Documents*. Westport, Greenwood Press, 1998.

Miles, Lendora Williams. Personal interview. *About Our People: The Black History of Malvern.* Malvern: Greater New Hope Baptist Church, 2000. 8-9.

Morrison, Toni. "The Talk of the Town." *New Yorker*

Murdoch, Alvin. Interview by Pam Uzzell. December 2010. Audio transcript.

National Newspaper Directory and Gazetteer. New York: Pettingill & Co., 1899.

"Origins at Tuskegee." *National Trust for Historic Preservation.* Web. 4 April 2011.

Parker, Larry. Interview by Pam Uzzell. April 2011. Audio transcript.

Patterson, Ruth Polk. *The Seed of Sally Good'n: A Black Family of Arkansas.* Lexington: The University Press of Kentucky, 1996. *xi*-xii.

Perry, M.R. "Negro Normal, Garland County. *Biennial Report of the State Superintendent of Public Instruction.* Little Rock: Arkansas Democrat Co., 1896.

Pierce, Judy. Interview by Pam Uzzell. December 2010. Audio transcript.

Raines, Robert. Interview by Foster Braun. *American Road Trip Talk Podcast.* 30 November 2011. Web audio. 5 May 2012.

Slave Narratives: A Folk History of Slavery in the United States from Interviews with Former Slaves, Arkansas Narrative, Part 6. Whitefish, MT: Kessinger, 2004. 27.

Smith, Kenneth L. *Sawmill: The Story of Cutting the Last Great Virgin Forest East of the Rockies.* Little Rock: University of Arkansas, 1986.

"State Listings for Arkansas." *National Register of Historic Places.* Web. 12 March 2010.

Stockley, Griff. *Blood in Their Eyes: The Elaine Race Massacres Of 1919.* Little Rock: University of Arkansas Press, 2004.

Sullivan, Geraldine. Interview by Ajuan Mance. December 2010. Audio transcript.

Taylor, Warren. Interview by Samuel S. Taylor. 1936-1938. *Arkansas Narratives.* Washington, D.C.: Works Progress Administration, 1941. *Project Gutenberg.* Web. 22 August 2010.

"The Arkansas Survey Report." *The Journal of the Arkansas Educational Association* 6.3-4 (1922).

The American Baptist Year-Book. Philadelphia: American Baptist Publication Society, Northern Baptist Convention, 1917.

The Black History of Malvern.

Warner, Charles Dudley. "Studies of the Great West, VII: Memphis and Little Rock." *Harpers,* 77 (1888): 429-439.

Wilkerson, Isabel. *The Warmth of Other Suns. The Epic Story of America's Great Migration.* New York: Vintage, 2011.

Willis, Jewell "Pete," Jr. Interview by Ajuan Mance. July 2010. Audio transcript.

—. Interview by Ajuan Mance. August 2011. Audio transcript.

Woods, J.B. "The Man Who Never Sold an Acre," *The Crisis* 14.1 (May 1917): 15-17.

Index

Football, A.A. Wilson Dragons, 40-42, 44-46, 48, 50-51, 77, 82, 84, 86-88
Football, Malvern Leopards, 16, 29, 31-36, 72, 102
Garland County, Arkansas, x, 5, 6, 19, 128
Graham, Tillie Yancy Benson, 92, 133-135
Great Migration, The, xii, 130-131
Greater New Hope Missionary Baptist Church, Malvern, 135
Green, Ed, 9, 10-12, 14-15, 111, 112
Green, Tolese, 49
Griffen, Dr. Patricia L. Greene, 94-95, 116
Griffin, Richard, 65, 95
Hall, Bishop Carruth, 95-96
Harley, Clint, 49
Harvey, Future Mae, 25-26
Hawkins, Jenny V., 30
Henry, Joan, 48-49, 50, 68
Henry, Lindsey, 48, 50-52
Henson, Taylor, 12-15, 54, 92, 132
Hill, John, 25-26, 42-46, 50-51, 86-88
Hill, Madre, 105
Hot Spring County, Arkansas, 6, 9, 20, 21, 30, 40, 92, 96, 102, 128
Hot Springs, Arkansas, vii, xi, 3-4, 5-6, 8, 13, 19, 80, 98, 115, 119-120, 127-129, 136-147
Hunter, Jimmy, 7, 25, 48-49, 51, 119. 120, 122-124
Hunter, Laura, 7-8, 10. 25, 26-28, 39-43, 52-53, 120-121
Jasper, Marva, 3, 7, 25
Johnson, Coach L., 66, 72
Jones, Billy Earl, 37,

Jones, Eutah and Viola, 57, 131-132, 135
Jones, Horace, 31, 72
Jones, X.L., 38, 112
Jordan, Gerald, 23, 38, 47-48, 96, 130-131
Knight, Nerissa Witherspoon, 105, 114, 116
Lambert, Wesley, 49
Lawson, Dr. Yolanda, 105-106
Lee, Tecola, 30
Lovelace, Yvonne D. English, 96
Lumber Industry, 2, 6, 8-11, 12, 15, 17, 99
Majorettes, Malvern Colored High School, 37
Malvern Avenue, Hot Springs, Arkansas, 141-142
Malvern Colored Elementary School, 21-28, 30, 37, 47, 67
Malvern Colored High School, viii-ix, xii, 30-37, 40, 47, 59, 64, 65, 66, 71, 72, 74, 89, 90, 92, 93, 98, 102, 107, 115, 123, 133
Malvern Senior High School, 33, 40, 45, 81-89, 97, 102-108, 110, 112-114, 115
Malvern Wilson Alumni Scholarships, 112-114
Merriweather, Alice Flanagan, 52
Merriweather, Hannah Jean, 37
Merriweather, Orrie Lee, 37
Miles, Lendora Williams, 3, 4, 21, 25, 55
Miller, Shag, 130-132, 135
Mitchell, Rev. Henry, vii, 40, 42, 44, 47, 50, 52, 85, 97, 124

166

About the Author

Ajuan Maria Mance is a Professor of English at Mills College in Oakland, California, where she holds the May Treat Morrison Chair in American History. She earned a B.A. in English with honors in creative writing from Brown University. She holds an M.A. and a Ph.D. in English from the University of Michigan, Ann Arbor. A 19th-century African American literature specialist, she is the author of *Inventing Black Women: African American Women's Poetry and Self-Representation, 1877-2000* (University of Tennessee Press, 2007).

About the Publisher

Based in Malvern, Arkansas, the Henson Benson Foundation was founded by area native Dr. Samuel Benson. Created in order to preserve and transmit the history and legacy of Malvern, Arkansas and surrounding communities, the Foundation also promotes and supports the educational aspirations and interests Malvern area youth through the contributions and advocacy of its public school alumni, community leaders, and local businesses.

In pursuit of these interests, the Henson Benson Foundation has adopted the following two-fold mission:

1. To promote knowledge, understanding, and appreciation for the history and legacy of Malvern, AR and its surrounding communities
2. To promote opportunities, aspirations, and achievements in educational endeavors for deserving learners

In order to achieve these ends, the Foundation has identified the following objectives:

- To explore the unique history of race relations in the Hot Springs/Garland County area and the legacy of their contributions to the region and beyond.
- To produce and disseminate educational materials about the social and economic history of the Malvern, Arkansas region, including the contributions of significant individuals in that history.
- To provide scholarship assistance to deserving students who demonstrate the potential to make a positive contribution to society.

- To provide financial support to the Malvern Wilson Alumni Committee for educational community activities.
- To support the Malvern-Tuggle Restoration Organization in its renovation of the Tuggle school as a multipurpose center for training and counseling students.

Henson Benson Foundation board members include: Samuel G. Benson, M.D., Ph.D. (Walnut Creek, CA), Bonnie Adams (Malvern, AR), Lillian Beard (Malvern, AR), Charlie Carroll (Malvern, AR), Larry Parker (Malvern, AR), Manuel Sanchez (North Hollywood, CA), and Jewell Willis (Malvern, AR).

Made in the USA
Middletown, DE
20 June 2023

33027800R00104